"When my wife and I first met Steve Musick, we had a quiet hunch that this man had something in his life that put him in a rare category. We could not figure it out until he shared all of his story with us. He is a man of unusual depth, care, honesty, and relational brilliance—qualities that I know come from what you will read about here. Having been invited to be his whole-life mentor, I trust his story in every detail. He relives his time with Jesus daily and shares it through every encounter he has with others. One caution: prepare for your own life to experience some welcome, needed change and growth as you encounter Jesus in these pages of deep truth and life-giving love."

> —WES ROBERTS, founder/master mentor, Leadership
> Design Group

"Scrap what you know about to-heaven-and-back stories. At least if the ones you know are silly and saccharine. Steven's account of his time in 'That Place' is raw, credible, and profound. Most important, it will inspire you to draw closer to God—and to fill earth with heaven's light."

> —DREW DYCK, senior editor of CTPastors.com
> and author of *Yawning at Tigers*

"As I read *Life After Heaven*. I ~~~~~~~~ he loss of my dear father-in-law ~~~~~~~~ ior in the coming world, a wor~ ~~~~~~~ even Musick. I found deep con ~~~~~~~~ account as I imagined my loved ones e ~~~~~~~ rich, saturated sensations and fathomless love and peace in heaven. But this book goes beyond just describing heaven. It encourages, energizes, and brings zest, power, and hope to us in the here and now. I find myself watching and waiting for 'bubbles of heaven,' the 'beautiful closeness of the kingdom of heaven,' to break through and change everything. This is a book of radical comfort and outrageous hope."

—LORILEE CRAKER, *New York Times*, CBA, and ECPA
best-selling author of *My Journey to Heaven* with Marv
Besteman and *Anne of Green Gables, My Daughter, and Me*

"People like Steven Musick telling of visits to heaven always raise my Missouri-bred skepticism. But I remember Paul's visit recounted in 2 Corinthians 12:1–9 or John's visit in the Revelation and look to the results of the story. Musick's is to make God's presence all the more real here on earth. He tells powerful stories, 'bubbles of heaven' times, when God's love meets earth's needs. There is much wisdom in the story: 'Poverty in God's kingdom . . . is tightly holding on to what you're supposed to give away.' The blandness of worldly living is overcome by the personal presence of God who is Emmanuel, promising 'Lo, I will be with you always.' Ponder prayerfully with Bible and heart open."

—GERRY BRESHEARS, professor of systematic theology,
Western Seminary, Portland

"I am fascinated with the stories of those who have experienced heaven, but I'm often left feeling disappointed after reading books of others' experiences of heaven. *Life After Heaven* certainly did not disappoint! Steven R. Musick's book left me feeling satisfied and renewed. I can truly say it's the very best book I've read on this topic, and I've read quite a few!"

—LINDSAY ANDREWS, Blogging for Books reviewer

"I am personally more interested in life before death than life after, but Steve has done a marvelous job bridging the two. I found this book relevant and helpful."

—WILLIAM PAUL YOUNG, author of *The Shack*

LIFE
AFTER
HEAVEN

STEVEN R. MUSICK

WITH PAUL J. PASTOR

LIFE AFTER HEAVEN

How My Time in Heaven
Can Transform Your
Life on Earth

WATERBROOK

LIFE AFTER HEAVEN

All Scripture quotations, unless otherwise indicated, are taken from the King James Version. Scripture quotations marked (ESV) are taken from ESV® Bible (the Holy Bible, English Standard Version®), copyright © 2001 by Crossway, a publishing ministry of Good News Publishers. Used by permission. All rights reserved. Scripture quotations marked (NIV) are taken from the Holy Bible, New International Version®, NIV®. Copyright © 1973, 1978, 1984, 2011 by Biblica Inc.® Used by permission. All rights reserved worldwide.

Certain names have been changed to protect the identity of the persons involved. Any resulting resemblance to real persons is coincidental and unintentional.

Trade Paperback ISBN 978-1-60142-988-9
eBook ISBN 978-1-60142-989-6

Copyright © 2017 by Steven R. Musick

Cover design by Kelly L. Howard

Published in the United States by WaterBrook, an imprint of the Crown Publishing Group, a division of Penguin Random House LLC, New York.

WATERBROOK® and its deer colophon are registered trademarks of Penguin Random House LLC.

The Cataloging-in-Publication Data is on file with the Library of Congress.

Printed in the United States of America
2017

10 9 8 7 6 5 4 3 2

SPECIAL SALES
Most WaterBrook books are available at special quantity discounts when purchased in bulk by corporations, organizations, and special-interest groups. Custom imprinting or excerpting can also be done to fit special needs. For information, please e-mail specialmarketscms@penguinrandomhouse.com or call 1-800-603-7051.

This book is dedicated to a lioness of a woman I met in 1975, married in 1978, and who is the only reason I am still alive today. She accepted a brainiac social dwarf when no one else would. Together we built lives of immeasurable depth and richness. Elaine J. Musick is a world-class lady. I believe she is an angel sequestered in a sack of skin, sent specially to rescue and complete me. She is a gift, pure and simple.

This book is my gift to her, as she is present in every page.

The two most important days in your life are the day you were born and the day you find out why.

—MARK TWAIN

CONTENTS

NOTE FROM PAUL J. PASTOR

I was on a writing retreat at a local abbey when my phone rang. It was a good friend who'd recently taken a job with the publishing house that released the book you now hold. "I have a project you might be interested in," he said. "But you need to hear me out. It's a heaven-and-back story."

If I hadn't known Andrew, I would have laughed and hung up. After all, he knew my feelings about what I call "heavenly tourism" books. While I think many of them are based on real experiences, the way they are told, in my experience, is overmarketed, wrongly focused only on "after you die," and (sorry) rather kitschy. I was skeptical.

But I knew and trusted Andrew. "Go on," I said.

"Well, I think you need to talk to Steve," he continued. "There's just . . . something about him."

With a little reluctance, I said yes. And after a couple of hour-long phone calls, I agreed. There was something about Steve, something honest and deep. Something kind and quietly magnetic. Not only did I feel his story of a near-death experience was credible enough to print, but it had an emphasis I'd never heard before in Christian stories of trips to heaven. It cared about here—the world we see now. And over the course of a few weeks, I realized I wanted to be the person to help him tell his story.

The point of Steve's story isn't divine escapism or "wait till you die for the pie in the sky." It expresses, through the story of one man's life and death and life again, one of my deepest theological beliefs: God's work in our world is something far greater than merely getting people to heaven; it is bringing heaven to earth in an open mystery, in a secret fullness. "Heaven is much closer than we've been led to believe," you'll hear Steve say often, both in his teaching and in his everyday conversation. And here is a story that illustrates that principle like no other I've ever heard in person.

During our time talking through his great experience, what impressed me most was the overwhelming sense that when Steve was relating his story beyond the white tunnel, he wasn't just telling it. He was remembering it. It was real. And it had changed everything about his life.

While making this book, I came to know and love Steve as a friend. Between spending long hours with black notebooks and tape recorders, we prayed together, ate together, laughed together, hiked to Oregon waterfalls, and drove curving highways together. We swapped stories of our families, work, and hobbies. We munched hamburgers and burritos. We talked fishing. He got to know my wife and kids and ate spaghetti at my table. He's a simple, everyday man. Easy to spend time with. But in each of those situations, my mind went back to Andrew's words: ". . . something about him."

It's true.

I think that "something" about Steve is heaven—not as a far-off reality but close. Closer than we've been led to believe. I hope you'll meet him someday and sense it for yourself.

I was skeptical about this story at first. Even as we arranged for my creative involvement, I was considering whether I wanted my name on this book. But that's not the case anymore. I'm proud to be associated with Steve's message.

In working with Steve to tell his story, I have become convinced that his account of That Place is worth wide attention, worth your attention. But further, I have felt and experienced for myself the power that comes with an awareness of the beautiful closeness of the kingdom of heaven. I am encouraged, not just for the hope and the clear presence of God beyond death, but for hope now. For hope in this life. Steve's remarkable story has helped make that more real to me than I had ever experienced before.

Truly, it has.

It's my prayer that it will do the same for you.

INTRODUCTION

My years on earth have been unusually defined by an experience in heaven. My years of life were critically influenced by my death—a death, by God's grace, that is proving well worth living for.

This great experience described in the following pages is actually very hard for me to talk about even now. In fact, it took me ten years to tell my wife about it and another twenty-five years to talk about it publicly. Part of the reason is that sharing this ignites in me a deep, indescribable desire to go back. Nothing—nothing—on this side of heaven equates to the kind of joy that you have being there. Once you've had that kind of experience, you don't want to be here. You want to go back there. You just do. And the desire to be there is so intense and so inexpressible that you feel guilty for not wanting to be present in your own life or with your own family. But I know that's not my call yet. One day. One day I will go back.

As a result of my experience, I no longer struggle at all with my faith. I have plenty of other struggles, but wondering if I'm saved is not one of them. In an unusual way, my faith became sight when I was thrown out of the tunnel of light and into the presence of Jesus, as you will soon read. There's a certainty for me that came with that experience. I know what it will be like when I go back. I have seen heaven. I know firsthand that the presence of Jesus is my home. I don't have to believe; I merely have to remember. It is still fully real to me. Perfectly fresh. And I know I will fully return there one day.

But even as I look forward to returning to That Place, I feel passionate and deeply called to be fully here in the meantime. As much as I long to return, it fuels me to see God's work and presence here, where we live and work and weep and play and receive tastes of his presence and of heaven. I want my life to be a preview of coming attractions. I want people around me to get a flash of heaven, a glimpse of what Jesus is like and what the Father is like.

I recognize the impossibility of recreating that perfect place on this imperfect earth. But I believe we should try. I know it is what we were made for and what all of us want. Everybody. God's kingdom can be seen in part now, even though the totality of that joy has to wait. You and I can see glimpses of it and can welcome the kingdom of heaven that Jesus preached so often about while he walked the earth.

We can feel it now. We can taste it now, even if it's not the full thing. "Thy kingdom come, Thy will be done in earth, as it is in heaven" (Matthew 6:10).

I think we're supposed to have that.

What's more, I think we can.

You don't have to have an experience like mine to truly experience some of the kingdom. You and I can feel it and know it now. We can even learn to anticipate such moments. I think my death can be one worth living for. I don't want this to sound arrogant, but I think this is why I'm here. Why I couldn't stay there. And why I'm supposed to tell you about it.

You see, this is not just a story of life after death.

This is a story of life after heaven.

PART 1

FROM EARTH
TO HEAVEN

A LIFE BEGUN

I'm sitting in a six-lane intersection close to home, my blue Subaru station wagon idling at the traffic light. Through the windshield I see a watery sun going down over the Colorado mountains, red and hazy in the summer sky.

A white moving van pulls up in the turning lane to my left. A white panel truck pulls up on my right. We wait for the light to change.

My vision is totally obscured by the two trucks, one on each side of me. The light clicks to green. The trucks don't move. *Are they texting or something?* I think. I step on the gas.

My car accelerates into the intersection just in time to meet a careening green-and-white garbage truck running a red light. The massive truck smashes into my driver's side post, tearing through my car, atomizing glass, crushing my body with a sickening crash. I am killed instantly.

I wake up from the dream.

It's the middle of a warm night in June 2011. My bedroom is dark; my heart pounds. The atmosphere in the room feels heavy, like a spiritual weight is pressing down on us. My wife, Elaine, wakes up instantly, feeling something significant has happened. "What was that?" she asks. Still disturbed, I tell her the dream. We fervently, earnestly pray together.

Lying there in the dark, we both have the overwhelming feeling the dream means something, something from God far too important to ignore. Somehow, we just know it.

For the next several weeks we prayed for him to tell us what to do, how to understand it. We were unnerved. We were inquisitive. But the interpretation didn't come. I didn't get it. So as the days went by as usual, we moved on as usual too.

But "usual" didn't last.

About three weeks later I pull up to a six-lane intersection. A watery sun descends over the Colorado mountains. The light is red, like blood or fire. A white moving van pulls up on my left. A white panel truck comes up on my right. I can't see past them.

I've been here before. My mind begins to tremble. Now I get it.

The light changes from blood red to green. The trucks stay put. I don't move. I start to count the seconds. One thousand one. Nothing. One thousand two. Nothing. One thousand three. Nothing. One thousand fou—. The green-and-white garbage truck comes from my left, runs the red light, rockets through the intersection with the sound of screeching metal. Then he's gone. Both white trucks move out.

I step on the gas and move through the intersection and then immediately pull over. I am nauseous, shaking. In my soul God speaks to me: *I could bring you back home anytime. I want you to get serious about telling your story.*

I took long, deep breaths, letting the oxygen calm me. I had wondered for years why I was alive (for reasons you're about to read). Conversations with my wife and friends, those close to me, were beginning to have a common theme: "I think God wants you to tell your story."

There, as the car idled by the road and my adrenaline slowly began to ebb, I knew they were right.

———

Denver, Colorado. The Mile-High City. A place of crisp mountain air and clear sunshine and ringed by mountains and alpine beauty. I was born here in 1956 at the height of the baby boom, part of an old Denver family.

My father bounced from job to job with long periods of unemployment in between. He always seemed unsettled in his world of work. My mother compensated for that, keeping herself constantly busy and largely unavailable. So even though they were there, they weren't really there for me.

I was the second of two boys, two years apart in age. We grew up essentially as latchkey kids during the times Dad was working. Taking advantage of my parents' physical and emotional vacancy, my older brother abused and tormented me relentlessly. He liked to beat the tar out of me just because he could. Since I had a lot of allergies as a boy, I received frequent injections. My brother would wait for me to get home, get me alone, and punch the injection sites as hard as he could, bruising them and causing them to swell. (Much later in his life, my brother was diagnosed with bipolar disorder, a diagnosis that now makes our troubled relationship understandable and forgivable.)

My brother was strong and fast, extraordinarily gifted in athletics. That ease of success, perhaps combined with the manic highs of his undiagnosed condition, made him the kind of person who could walk into a room and immediately become the focus of attention. All eyes naturally went to him, like a star athlete walking through his high school. In he would stride, and *whoomp*. All the air in the place would be sucked out. But because of his serious behavioral issues, he was a handful for my mom and dad. My mother didn't know how to deal with him, and my dad was just passive, always trying to smooth things over and make peace.

Because I wasn't particularly athletic or talented, I couldn't compete for attention in the shadow of my brother. I was a good student, though, so I found my identity in being a brainiac, which, let's face it, doesn't lead to the same kind of recognition or popularity as athletic prowess. So my early life was defined by being invisible.

I was just a kid. Life was what it was, and I learned to get by.

I bear no malice for the way I was raised. I have no issues with my brother today. Nor do I have any with my mother or father. They're in heaven now, and we experienced healing in our relationship later in life. In many ways, even in spite of the vacancy and violence I experienced, our family life was rich. I never doubted my parents loved and cared about me. They just didn't know how to manage a household with a son who was so needy. Looking back, I can't imagine being in their shoes. It must have been a tremendous challenge.

And what my parents lacked in emotional depth, they made up for in spiritual depth. Clearly, God was working from the very beginning. We were orthodox Episcopalians, deeply involved in our parish community at Christ the King Episcopal Church. I accepted Christ when I was seven, though in hindsight I realize I didn't understand the depth of what that commitment meant. I went through catechism, was an altar boy, and always loved being in church. When Father Kempsel, the rector of our parish, needed an acolyte on Easter, he chose me. That was huge. I felt safe there. I felt seen. I felt recognized.

One of the most important memories of my childhood is when my mom was in the hospital for a major surgery and my dad was out of work. Father Kempsel came over one evening. I listened from the stairs while he sat in the kitchen with my dad. "Chuck," the priest kindly said, "we've missed your tithe for the last three months. That's not like you. I'm concerned. Is everything okay?"

The rector didn't know it, but my father had just made us lunch for the following day, using all the food we had left in the house. My dad explained that we didn't have any income because of Mom's illness and his unemployment.

"Now I understand," Father Kempsel said with compassion. They prayed together, and the rector left. My dad sat at the kitchen table with his head in his hands and wept. The next day my brother and I left for school with the minimal lunch my father had prepared. There was nothing more in the house.

I came back that afternoon, though, and there was food everywhere. The pantry was full! So was the fridge. Overjoyed, I dunked Oreo cookies in cold milk and ate and ate.

I learned later that the rector's discretionary fund was the source of the abundance. The local parish provided sacks of food for our family at that time of need, along with the promise of more if it was needed. That was a powerful moment, because for the first time I connected what we did in church on Sunday with the rest of the week. I connected faith to life. I understood that's the way the kingdom should be. Sunday was important, but it wasn't all-important. Ensuring we had food to eat on Friday was every bit as important to our church family as worship on Sunday. We were part of a community.

When I was a kid, my faith roots began to go deep. However, at that time of my life, I probably equated knowing God with Bible knowledge. I knew about God, but I didn't really know God. My dad raised us by reading Scripture at bedtime. My father, so kind, gentle, and attentive when my brother wasn't there, created a safe space with just him and me during those evening times. These were the moments I felt most loved and accepted. I loved reading Bible stories with him. Heroes like Joseph, Daniel, David, and Jesus fascinated me. I wanted to be those guys, to see the miracles they saw, to be part of a great story.

I thought I had a good sense about who Jesus was. I read my Bible, so I knew Jesus was full of love. I saw that he was courageous, that he worked and had a calling, and that he loved kids. I knew he was the spitting image of God, his Father. With all that said, my faith wasn't really experiential or relational or intimate. God felt distant, impersonal. I didn't think people could have a relationship with him any more than they could with George Washington or anyone else I had read about. I didn't really sense he cared about me in any personal way or cared about having a relationship with me. He was real and loving but far off. How could I really matter to him personally? Why would he even notice me? I wondered if my story really mattered at all to him. I knew him a little. Did he know me?

Likewise, I thought being a Christian meant going to church, being good. There were rules to follow, and I was always good at following rules. There were behaviors I assumed you adopted to be members of God's family.

I recognized heaven as a reality, but it felt really distant. It didn't affect my here and now or my everyday world. I had my "fire insurance," my "ticket." I knew in my mind exactly where I was headed when I died. I just didn't think much about it. Why would I? I thought of earth and heaven as totally separate places. Heaven? It was that end-of-the-road place you went when you died.

———

As we grew into our high school years, my brother no longer beat me the way he did when we were younger. But even though the physical abuse let up, I still carried emotional bruises.

Part of the fallout was that I had virtually no identity, no sense of self-worth. Because attention usually had gotten me punched at home, I had become a chameleon who worked to blend into the background. Being quiet was the easy thing. My brother loved the attention, so I let him have it. All of it. Like my father, passivity became my method of coping. I simply tried not to be noticed, and it largely worked. But it came at a cost. I was a social dwarf in many ways because of this, finding it difficult to connect with friends or build relationships with kids my age. I went through adolescence without feeling recognized.

There was one glorious exception. During my growing-up years, my family lived close to Dad's parents, who wonderfully loved me and made me feel seen. In fact, we were close enough for me to ride my bike to their house over on West Seventy-Third Place. I was the youngest of their thirteen grandkids, but they still saw me for who I was and really cared. My grandfather was one of the most important people in my life. His home became a refuge for me, and I spent lots and lots of simple, quiet time with my grandfather George. We would talk about everything and anything. I felt I had a special place in my grandparents' house.

I loved my grandfather's quiet but kind ways—putting out birdseed, journaling, going to a special room he called his "womb room," set aside for quietness and rejuvenation. In him I saw an example of hard work and craftsmanship, of benevolence and generosity, of making provision for those around him with his powerful God-given talents. He was an architect and also incredibly gifted with finances. He told me, "Money is only good for what it can do for others." And he lived that out for a lifetime and beyond through his legacy and values passed down to others.

———————

Until the summer after my junior year, I wasn't much to look at, especially next to my athletic older brother. But that year I shot up to five feet eleven. I became a man almost overnight—and a strong, healthy one at that. When I returned for my senior year of high school, people I'd known for years didn't recognize me because my appearance had changed so much. Having already earned enough credits to graduate, I stuck around that school for only two weeks, trying to convince them to let me graduate early so I could work. Finally I did.

Over the next several months, I earned enough money as a gofer errand boy at a downtown firm to pay for a year of college. I didn't know where I'd get the funds for subsequent years, but I figured I'd deal with that when the time came. I didn't feel comfortable taking out student loans, and I didn't know anything about scholarships. I assumed I'd go for a year and see what options presented themselves.

So in the fall of 1974, I left for the University of Colorado. I moved what little bit of stuff I owned into the college dorm by myself because my parents were once again focused on my brother. And, as many college kids do, I entered that new phase of life and pretty much left my faith behind. I wasn't rebelling against it, but it seemed to have little relevance.

Being a brainiac may not have served me well socially, but it did academically. I had gotten a thirty-five out of thirty-six on my college board tests, and with that momentum I had tested out of two full years of my university program—all my general courses in science, physics, chemistry, and so on.

Other than my finances, I had it all planned out. I wanted to be a rural pediatrician, practicing medicine for a small town somewhere. I had convinced myself that the bachelor life was for me. I was prepared to be married to my work.

Yeah, I had it all figured out. Until I met Elaine.

She showed up midsemester and moved in down the hall in my dormitory. She was working on the prerequisites for physical therapy school. And chemistry was giving her trouble. She needed a tutor.

After one look at her, I became a chemistry expert.

She was driven and focused. Nothing was going to distract her from achieving her goals. But soon our tutoring sessions included unconventional study methods, like catching a movie or going to a party. We built a romance to fit between our studies like the grout between bathroom tiles—not much to look at initially, but it held our relationship together. Solid. She was the longest relationship I had ever had, but anything longer than a week would have set that record.

We'd walk to the recreation center on campus. She would go swimming, and I would head to the basketball courts. I remember finishing early one Saturday and simply sitting in the viewing center and watching her glide across the pool. She lifted herself out of the pool, smiled, and waved. I just gawked and weakly waved back.

"What?" she asked.

"Oh . . . nothing," I answered. That wasn't entirely true. But what would I have said? "You're simply spectacular"? "You're sweeping my heart away"? Or maybe the clincher: "I don't want to graduate and just be married to my work anymore. I want to be married to you."

It would be a while before I would speak those thoughts. But in those months Elaine's presence gently changed the course of my life. If I had executed my original plan, I'd be a very lonely and miserable doctor today. While there was certainly testosterone involved, something much deeper was going on inside. Little did I know just how integral this new relationship would become. But even less did I suspect how much my life was about to change.

―――――

My school funds ran out after that first year, right on schedule.

"I can't afford to stay here at the university, Elaine."

"You're dropping out?"

"I have to. There's no money."

I had no idea, but I was standing at one of the most significant crossroads of my life.

2

THE RELUCTANT VOLUNTEER

I didn't want to be in the military. But I just didn't see I had any alternatives at that point.

I went to my dad, who had been an infantry grunt, for advice. After our less-than-encouraging conversation about my options, I decided to be proactive. I'd enlist in the military, pick my own job, and try to make the best of it.

I knew the army wasn't my first military choice. I had a fear of heights, so the air force? Probably not. That left the navy. Having been born and raised in Denver, I had never seen the ocean. My family was just slightly above the poverty level, and we'd had only two vacations during my entire upbringing. But I'd watched movies like *In Harm's Way* with John Wayne and Kirk Douglas and fallen in love from afar with the sea. It looked exciting. The navy also had unique educational opportunities for a sailor's time in the service, so I went to the recruiting office.

After I'd taken the requisite tests there, the recruiter reviewed my scores. "What are you doing here? Why aren't you in school?" he chided. "These are really good scores!"

"I'm out of money for college," I said.

"Okay," he laughed. "Well, you can probably qualify for any school I have."

I qualified for the duty station of a combat information center, the nerve center of a battle fleet. I picked that as my "A" school since it virtually guaranteed I'd be placed on an aircraft carrier, where I could enroll in the navy's scholarship-at-sea program and finish my college degree aboard ship. My plan was to finish my enlistment, use the GI Bill for a master's degree, and go from there. I could finish my education while serving, and the navy would pay for it. I thought it was a great plan. So I joined.

Elaine was surprised—and a little dismayed—about my decision to enlist. "Don't you have any other choices?" she asked. But without money for school and no other employment opportunities on the horizon, I really didn't. I was trying to make the best of a tough situation.

So I left for recruit training in November 1975. I boarded a train at Denver's historic Union Station and left for Naval Station Great Lakes in Chicago, Illinois. Elaine, my grandmother and grandfather, and my mom and dad came to see me off. They all saluted smartly at me from the platform.

They had no way of knowing that the nineteen-year-old kid they knew, waving back at them from the window of the train, would be gone forever.

That kid never returned.

———

The trip went smoothly, and I arrived at boot camp. Accustomed to gauging my surroundings, I paid careful attention to this new setting. From the first I saw that if someone excelled in the military, he would be recognized. Rank, service, medals—recognition is huge. Having grown up with virtually no recognition, I wanted to do well. And I believed I could.

That first week I sensed I had a choice to make: I could be only one of two people—a man who blended in with my background, as I had for my entire life, or one who stood out from it. With some effort I made a conscious decision to excel, to be distinctively different. So far I had lived my life being plain vanilla, vacant. I didn't want to be that person anymore. Here was a turning point—a chance at freedom, an opportunity to become the person I had always longed to be. I welcomed the clean slate and planned to give it my very best. I wanted to lead, to make a difference. I was ready to be noticed.

As it turned out, I thrived in the military. I had become a very strong young man at 195 pounds. Solid. In the first four weeks of the very physical camp training, no one had been able to knock me off my feet, including the impressive six-foot-three recruit in charge of our unit, who was a wrestler and destined for the submarine corps. He outweighed me by a good fifty pounds. Although I wasn't selected to be a leader in boot camp, I was a guy people respected. And I loved it. Long gone were the days of being picked on or ignored. Throughout November all went well for me, though the training intensified.

My absence made Elaine and me grow fonder of each other. We wrote two or three letters a week to each other. The highlight of boot camp was hearing "Mail call!" I didn't need to rummage around to know if I had mail. They would open the mailbag, and all seventy-two guys in my company would smell the Chantilly perfume Elaine had sprayed on her letters to me. "Musick!" they'd scream. "You gotta tell her to quit doing this!" I asked her to stop. So she started spraying them twice.

———

One day in the first week of December, we were eating lunch in the chow hall. As always, nearly a thousand people were there, eating as fast as they could to get every needed calorie before the bell rang and any uneaten food had to be left behind. The cacophony of clattering plates and silverware and hungry sailors eating everything in sight filled the chow hall.

Four SEALs—the navy's top troops—walked in. The respect they commanded was unlike anything I had ever seen. These four navy men stood there in their fatigues—not even their dress blues—on the stage overlooking the chow hall, and one of them simply cleared his throat. "Ahem."

The room immediately fell silent. They had everyone's complete attention, even the line officers', who dined in a different section of the hall. All eyes turned to the man. All ears attuned. After a nod from the officer in charge, the SEAL simply said, "SEAL training at 1800 hours. Anyone interested in qualifying for SEALs meet us at the aqua center." The four of them snapped to attention, nodded to the line officers, and walked out. Every-body went back to eating. I sat for a moment and looked at my plate.

That sounds like fun, I thought. *I think I'll try it.*

At 6:00 p.m. I walked through the frigid Illinois air to the aqua center with about thirty other recruits. The SEALs were waiting, poised with the kind of ready patience the toughest men in the world can afford to have. Then, with a few barked orders, the tests began.

"Into the pool!"

Fully clothed, we dove into the water. My heavy fatigues clung to my body, holding back my strokes. I swam as I'd never swum before, my heart racing. I swam to prove something, but I couldn't have said what. In the aqua center the echoes of dull splashes and pants for air echoed off the concrete and lapping water.

"Out of the pool, sailors!"

Water pouring off us, we climbed out of the pool. Our endur-ance was pushed as we began a regimen of push-ups and sit-ups and pull-ups and dips in our still-wet clothes. Fun this wasn't, but I was making it.

"Now let's see a little movement, boys!" The SEALs then ran us ragged back and forth between the pool and the gymnasium.

"Warmed up yet? Good. Let's cool you down."

We pulled on our boondockers—combat boots—and were turned back out onto the grinder.

"One mile. Six minutes. Go."

With that, off we charged, dripping wet, into the ten-degree weather of a Chicago December. My soaked trousers froze stiff in the first hundred yards. But I ran my very best. And I made it.

Only three of us were left after that frigid mile. When I walked back into the aqua center, the warmth of the air hit me like a humid wall. And the warmth wasn't just a physical sensation. Those same brusque SEALs who had just subjected us to torturous tests over the past hours now displayed an unexpected kindheartedness toward the three of us who had passed their test. They had laid out fresh, clean, warm clothes for us. "Here, get out of those wet clothes," one said as he held out a dry towel for me. I was surprised by the kindness in his eyes, and I welcomed this new sense of camaraderie.

While we dressed, they told us what the SEALs—the most elite members of the United States Navy—were like. If we decided to go for SEAL training, we would go to San Diego. "You think this was tough? It's just a taste of what the training's all about. We take only the best of the best. You're qualified to come and try out. You might not make it, sure. But if you do? It's the best job you'll ever have."

If we wanted to try out, we would leave recruit training after completing boot camp and go to San Diego. There the real tests would begin.

We were sitting on the floor, and the SEALs pulled us up by the hand. "You're tough. You've got sand, sailor," one said to me. It felt really, really good to know that I, who had felt overlooked for so long, was being seen. To know that I was good enough to become something more—to move on to the next step of something so difficult. It was the first time I knew I could be something special physically. I couldn't help thinking, *I'd like to see my brother take me on now.*

As I walked to my barracks, I thought back over the surreal evening. There had been more than nine hundred people in that chow hall. Thirty had shown up for the test. Only we three had made it through to the next level. But I knew what the SEALs said was right—only a few who enter SEAL training are able to finish. And if I was weeded out, I would lose my "A" school, my scheme for education on an aircraft carrier, all the plans I'd carefully laid out to that point. I wasn't willing to risk it. So I declined mentally. I wouldn't go to San Diego.

I didn't know then that my plans were about to all go awry anyway.

In my third week of training, we were marched into a classroom for a battery of academic tests. Two weeks later, in mid-December, I received a message to go to battalion headquarters. I had a lot of trepidation. *I don't know how, but I must have screwed up big time,* I thought. *What did I do?* As I marched to headquarters, I recounted what kind of trouble I could possibly be in.

My company commander sat in the waiting area. He glared at me, his eyes like laser beams slicing me in half. I didn't even sit down but stood at attention. The yeoman motioned me toward the open door. We walked immediately into the battalion commander's office. My company commander snapped to attention—something I hadn't seen before—and we waited.

The battalion commander sat at his desk, my military-records folder in front of him. He flipped it open and then looked at the company commander.

"Annapolis *and* SEALs?" he shouted. "This is not something I need to be hearing from up the chain of command! The commander of recruit training just chewed me out."

He turned to me. "What in the h— are you doing in recruit training?"

I didn't yet understand what he was talking about. So I repeated my now-familiar story. "Well, sir, after a year of college, I ran out of money and—"

The commanding officer stared at me, and with a wave of his hand, he said, "Your test scores are off the charts. After you finish recruit training and your 'A' school, you're not headed to the fleet. You're going to Annapolis, to the Naval Academy." He cocked his head. "And SEALs?" His eyes glimmered. "Do you play football? I hope so. We're really tired of our navy team getting kicked around."

He looked at us both. "You're dismissed," he said.

My head was spinning. My plan had just changed. They paid for your education at Annapolis, and you graduated as an officer. They had family quarters. Elaine and I could get married! *This is paradise,* I thought. The best thing that ever could have happened.

A battalion of nine hundred recruits. Three qualified for SEALs. Two for Annapolis. Only one qualified for both: me. I couldn't even recognize myself in my own life.

As we walked out, my company commander was steaming mad about being dressed down by his superior officer. "One of these days, I'll have to salute your a—," he spat. "But for the next eight weeks, your a— is mine."

———

I'm not recounting all this to be arrogant, to flex old muscles, or to impress you. It felt really good, but even then it didn't turn to pride, at least not as I remember it. Maybe because it was all so surreal, as if I were living someone else's life.

I see now that those brief weeks were God's encouragement to a young man who was struggling deeply inside. He was telling me, someone who had never believed it before, that I was capable. That I was special. That it was good for me to be visible, and that I was done with hiding. He was telling me that he saw me, that others saw me, and that I was worth seeing. For the first time in my life I felt like a man. He was telling me all this through circumstances.

One week later they told the battalion to stand in a line and roll up our sleeves.

3

A SHOT IN THE ARM

As part of recruit training, sailors are constantly being vaccinated against every mean and nasty bacteria and bug around the globe. Usually, the corpsmen (enlisted medical specialists) responsible for administering the injections come to your compartment and give you a dose right by your bunk. You get used to the routine: stand up, roll up your sleeve, let your arm dangle, don't move. They shoot the inoculation—*thoomp*—straight through the skin, no needles involved.

This day in mid-December 1975, the beginning of week five of training, was different. They herded hundreds of us—maybe as many as two thousand—into a hangar used for indoor training when the Chicago weather was worse than its typical awful. Corpsmen were running everywhere among the throng of sailors.

"You know the drill," someone yelled. "Inoculation time! Dress, right, dress! Roll up your sleeve! Hang!"

We followed orders. All over that hangar came the *thoomp* of inoculations, fast as popcorn. Then mine came. *Thoomp* into my arm. And the corpsman kept on shooting down the line.

I knew something was very wrong right away. Inside of two minutes I was in deep trouble. I flushed red all over. I began coughing.

I didn't know it yet, but fluid was filling my lungs. I didn't even ask to leave ranks but bolted for the bathroom. I made it barely in time to vomit what felt like two gallons of liquid into a urinal. I passed out on the floor.

I woke up a day later in the dispensary, on the recruit-training side of the naval base. I felt like a truck had run over me. I hurt everywhere. I was thirsty, like I'd been in a desert. Still dazed, I got up and began to wander, looking for water, any water at all. I ran into a corpsman on my way to the latrine. "What happened to me?" I managed to say through the haze.

"You and a lot of other people had a reaction to that shot," he said. "We pumped you full of epinephrine. Dried you out. No wonder you're thirsty. Get your water and go back to your compartment. You're okay."

I didn't know it yet, but I was carrying the live virus for the swine flu inside me. Besides that, I heard after the fact that I'd had an allergic reaction to the vaccine. Still later I learned that the government, panicked about a flu pandemic, had contracted with a Chicago laboratory to develop a swine flu vaccine in 1975. They needed a test bed for the shot. We were conveniently placed and couldn't say no. Both the soldiers at Fort Sheridan and the sailors at Great Lakes were inoculated with the new vaccine.

The new vaccine did not work well. I was told it was the first time since World War II that the Great Lakes Naval Hospital was full.

But at that moment I wasn't thinking about much besides how terrible I felt. "There were a lot of people we couldn't stabilize here," the corpsman said. "We had to take them to the hospital. I guess you and a whole bunch of others got hit hard."

Ugh. I guessed so too. I found water and guzzled it down in grateful gulps. I sort of returned to myself and then went back to my quarters.

I improved enough to finish recruit training, but I never got well. For the rest of my time at boot camp, I was constantly sick, fluid always sloshing around in my lungs. A heavy, wet cough clung to me like soaked clothing. I battled the swine flu—a bad, big-time flu—for the balance of my recruit training and the early part of "A" school.

There were people in the hospital even months later, and they had all kinds of ancillary issues tied to the swine flu. Somebody had really screwed something up. Hospital staff informed me later that the initial formulation of the vaccine they gave us was too strong. This was big, but it wasn't addressed by our commanding officers or the navy in any way. They never addressed it other than an oblique acknowledgment of it in the release of liability I would eventually sign upon my discharge.

Finally December was almost over. I was allowed to go home on leave for Christmas, still coughing but excited about my experiences with the SEALs and the plans to attend the academy. My family and Elaine celebrated with me, but they knew something wasn't right.

"You're coughing a lot," Elaine said when we were finally alone. "I'm worried about you."

"My parents have been saying that too," I said and shrugged. "But I'm fine. Really, I am."

She just stared.

"Seriously, it's just a nagging cold."

It wasn't, of course. My respiratory issues didn't get better. But I ignored it, thinking I would eventually recover.

I had an important conversation during that holiday leave. Elaine and I met with her dad, a strong man who loved his only daughter and youngest child. The words came out straight from my heart: "I want to marry your daughter."

I told him about Annapolis and then said, "They don't let you marry in the first year, but in the second they provide family housing, and the timing would be perfect. Elaine will have finished physical therapy school by then."

Her dad hesitated. Then he delivered the last thing I wanted to hear: "I do not give you permission to marry my daughter."

My heart beat faster somehow even as it sank.

"It's too much change," he went on. "That's over a year and a half away. There's a lot of uncertainty. I need to be sure you can take care of my little girl. I'm just not ready to give you my consent."

I turned to Elaine, and our eyes met. "Okay," I said, wanting to honor him. "But this just postpones it." I went on, looking back at her dad, "I'm not done asking."

Our happy Denver Christmas passed, and my leave in Colorado faded like a cut evergreen. I went back to Great Lakes and finished my recruit training. Then in February I went to my "A" school just across the railroad station in the same location. It was to be a fourteen-week program for the combat information center training I had signed up for.

The weeks marched by, but I didn't get well. Fits of coughing often interrupted a conversation or a laugh. And they came more frequently, feeling deeper and deeper in my wet lungs. Our classes, many of which dealt with sensitive military technology, were in closed environments, and at least half of the students were chain smokers. My compromised respiratory system couldn't handle the secondhand smoke. I worsened and then worsened more. My studies went great, but my health declined seriously.

Eventually the school transferred me to better quarters with four nonsmoking sailors. I had a predictable routine and liberty for the weekends. I enjoyed it. But I never felt good.

Then, on April 9, my lingering sickness took another downward turn. I felt awful, and for the first time I feared something was seriously wrong. I checked into the emergency room of the base hospital.

I must have looked as bad as I felt. The nurse behind the

counter took one look at me and ushered me directly into a treatment area, ahead of everyone else waiting for care. Within minutes three people were poking me and prodding me and pinching my fingernails.

"Stridor in respiration. Lips are cyanotic," one nurse noted to another and then looked at the doctor.

"We're going to find out what's wrong with you," the doctor told me, touching my left forearm in a fatherly gesture.

"I think you'll discover I have swine flu," I rasped, attempting a humorous tone. Although I hadn't officially heard of anyone else being given that diagnosis yet, the scuttlebutt among fellow ailing sailors was that we had been accidentally infected by the overly potent live vaccine.

Then I coughed again, and the levity left. All three medical professionals took a giant step back, recoiling as if I were contagious. The doctor leaned forward, still keeping his distance. "Were you on base in December?" he asked.

"Yes, sir. Over on the recruit side."

"So you got the shot?" he asked.

"Yes sir!"

"Were you transferred here to the hospital?"

"No sir. I was in the dispensary overnight."

"And you have been sick ever since?"

"Yes sir. But not this sick."

The doctor turned to the nurses and started barking all kinds of orders in that clipped, calmly urgent tone that disturbs a patient more than shouting would. "Start an IV. Pull a blood sample—I want a full series. I want a chest x-ray and an EKG. And arterial blood gases. And I want to know what his P02 counts are."

They went to work. Forty-five minutes later a different nurse strode in with a syringe in hand. "I'm going to give you a dose of aminophylline. It should clear up those clogged airways," she said.

As she readied me for the injection, my attention diverted to the music playing on the radio. I could hear Electric Light Orchestra's hit song "Evil Woman." I should have known something was about to come undone as I heard the lyrics "You took my body and played to win."

She flicked the syringe to get all the bubbles to the top and then pushed the plunger until liquid squirted out like champagne. She inserted the tip of the syringe into my IV tube. "This will fix you right up," she said as she depressed the plunger.

What came next happened about as fast as it takes to read this. My right arm felt hot. Heat started at the IV insertion point in my wrist, rushed down to my fingertips, rose back to my wrist, and climbed up my arm—red, racing, burning, beating. I didn't know I was allergic to aminophylline, and neither did they. And they had just administered a lethal dose directly into my bloodstream.

When the fire got to my chest, everything went black.

4

THE GREAT
EXPERIENCE

I am weightless.
Bodiless.

All around me a white tunnel of bright light sparkles.

I am here long enough to notice I am moving, flying at an incredible speed.

I feel as if I'm going somewhere.

Then, all of a sudden, I'm hurtled out of the tunnel into That Place.

I had been weightless going through the tunnel, but here on the other side, it's as if there's gravity. I walk normally. I have a body, and what's more, it's my body. And more than that, it's working and breathing fine. No burning chest. No fluid in my lungs.

I stand in a rolling green meadow. A massive, shady oak tree stands in the foreground, surrounded by a waist-high field of grass. A farmer would probably look at the heavy stalks and think it's time to put up the hay. A lush valley drops away to my left. I see a forest and rolling hills beyond, bounding the meadow.

There are billowy clouds and bright sunshine everywhere.

The light is brilliant, beyond description. I can see no roads or other construction. I am surrounded by a profound sense of abundance. Of completeness. Of perfect being. Everything is astonishingly bright.

I barely know how to describe the vibrancy of it all. It's like super high-definition television on steroids. Everything is crystal clear. The colors are indescribably rich. The photographic beauty of John Fielder's or *National Geographic's* famous images and the sharpness of Ansel Adams prints all pale in comparison to what I see as I simply look around in That Place. The visual experience overwhelms me.

I hear singing. This place is full of song! But it's in the background, as if the song is part of the fabric of the environment, driving the background of experience but never overwhelming it. It is simply there. Like the deep bass lines of a glorious symphony, the music swells and supports and envelops and complements. It is part of the very fabric of this reality. It's not a specific tune; instead, the music is simply part of everything. I can see no particular source for it. It just seems to be everywhere. The music is deep, resonant. There is a weight to it. And—how can I describe it?— it's like 20/20 hearing, perfectly sensed. I hear everything clearly. I hear birds and bugs (though I don't see any of either) and all the natural noises of being outdoors. I see no other people, no spirits or angels, though I suppose the voices in the music must come from someone.

The smells are pungent, even piercing. The vibrancy of every aroma is incredible, beyond words.

All these senses take me, envelop me, overcome me. But it is the emotional touch of the place that carries away my very heart. As a boy, my brother had once thrown me into a cedar toy chest and sat on the lid of that horrible box for an entire afternoon. I have been claustrophobic ever since. I don't like feeling closed in, so perhaps that is why this part of the experience affects me so deeply. I feel as if I am in a vise grip, held tight, yet with no fear, no powerlessness, no claustrophobia.

It is a perfect paradox of heaven: I feel absolutely held and absolutely free. I am physically feeling God's security. The safest place imaginable is in the arms of the Father. Once you've felt that, it's all you want. Nothing else, from that day to this, satisfies. It is the overwhelming, wonderful sensation of being held. Held in a tight grip, the way a strong parent lovingly hugs a child. Held tight, yet still completely free and secure.

Emotionally, being in This Place feels like being inside pure joy. There are simply no words to describe it, to create a context for understanding it. Language, vocabulary is simply too limiting. This Place defies depiction.

I am in a place of explosive peace—another paradox. Peace pursues you, lives and moves toward you, around you. There is no ebb or flow to the harmony. It is an ocean without tides. It's just there. In the same way that my vision is vibrant and the smells are pungent and the sounds are soothing and wonderful, this peace explodes at me. It's not passive in any way. It comes for me. This peace is not just a lack of conflict; it's something at a deep level that reassures all is well, everything is okay.

I feel relationship, as if I am someone's child. I feel like a son. This is a sense of home—true home—and total acceptance and belonging. My heart leaps. This is what I was made for! It is not at all foreign. It feels so right, so natural.

This Place must be heaven. This Place—heaven—is physical, real. In fact, it's more physical and real than the world I have known. It's not an ethereal, disembodied state, as some people might think. Senses, all my senses, are brilliant and deep. There is weight. There is movement. My body feels an overwhelming sense of freedom. It is wonderful. Totally free.

Heaven, through every sense, commands me to be present in the moment, in the now. There, in the richness and natural beauty, I don't think about the past. The idea of "future" has no meaning. Feeling so captivated by that sense of "now," I don't want to be anywhere else. All I want to do is stay here, right here. In the present.

I don't have any sense of the before, though it isn't as if my life before coming here is gone or erased. I am just totally present, totally joyful, totally here. Having been flung out of the tunnel with so much force into this perfect place leaves me no room to think about the "Evil Woman" or her fateful syringe in the emergency room. I have no sense of remorse, no sense of regret, no sense of loss. I'm not thinking about Elaine or never seeing my parents again or anything other than being here.

I stand in the meadow and think I must be dead. But joy floods over me. If this is the end, I'm liking it!

Oh, this is good. I feel it more deeply than anything I have felt before. This is the finish line.

Time has very little meaning in This Place, so I won't say that I looked around for any particular amount of time. I was able to take it all in, experience it all at once.

Immediately, a strong arm grabs me around the shoulders in a tight hug. "Welcome," says the most beautiful voice I have ever heard. "Walk with me."

It's Jesus Christ, the Son of God.

I just know it.

Jesus is a young man. I'd judge him to be about thirty-five years old. Clearly a man. He's a person. Not a shadowy figure, no figment of my imagination, not translucent or some floating being. A person. Solid. Shoulder-length dark brown hair. Dark hazel eyes that are soothing, reassuring. You would almost think he's a body builder. He is muscular and stocky, with a working man's body. He looks like someone who would be pulling on oars or who had been a logger.

He has angular features, strong and powerful. But for all his strength, his mannerisms and movements are the epitome of gentleness. He, like so much of heaven, is a paradox. Of course he would be. He is radiant. He shines, but that word isn't quite right. Glows might be better. There is a certain light about his countenance.

His hands are large and powerful, strong and supple, yet they are soft to the touch. No calluses. He wears a white robe with sleeves that fall only to his midforearm. He has a white rope, like a monk's belt, tied around his waist. He wears simple brown sandals on his feet.

"Welcome."

He has a tenor voice, soothing and melodic. A conversational voice. Not a monotone, but stable in timbre. Consistent. There's a soothing quiet to his voice. I feel immediately that the songs and music in the background are to highlight something else—the words of Jesus. His words are like the melody that the rest of the symphony supports. His words aren't just in the foreground of attention; they *are* the foreground of attention.

"Walk with me."

We set off walking together through the fields of This Place. He has an arm around me, the same way my grandfather did when I was seventeen. We walk through the deep meadows, the hayfields, stalks of the long grasses running through our hands. Jesus is passionate; there is a kind fierceness to him, truly the heart of the Lion of Judah.

But here is a surprise—we spend all our time together talking about me. He reviews my life to that point from a perspective totally beyond the human. He tells me everything—not only what happened to me as a little kid but why. And it is all okay. He tells me about my life as a teenager, and it is okay. He tells me what just happened to me in the navy, in the hospital. And it is okay. His words reveal there is purpose behind it all, a plan woven through my life. It gives meaning to every moment of it. And it is okay.

Even though I had felt as though I was all alone for most of my life, I hadn't been. The vacancy that I thought surrounded me was an illusion. God was there—is there—the whole time and there with purpose. I had no idea. I see it now. I see God's presence in my life. His hand guiding, providing, redeeming, protecting. Everything that happened to me is, in the end, a benefit.

———

I don't think I can transcribe our conversation word for word, but Jesus clearly and specifically reviews so many wounds in my life. In each situation he mentions, his words are like oil or salve, healing a place where I had been hurt or broken. Some of those wounds had been so deep that they were still open and festering. Many of the things he mentions hadn't struck me as a wound until he speaks about them. As we talk, I begin to understand the importance, the weight of things that many people would consider little hurts or cares. I begin to see my life from the perspective of heaven. And how different it looks.

I begin to understand my mother from a completely different perspective. Why she was the way she was. And Jesus makes it okay. I understand my father and why he had been so passive in the face of my brother's brutal actions. Jesus lays it out. And he makes it okay.

Jesus knows my family, my mother, my father—all of us so

intimately. He tells me about the work he is doing inside their lives. Everything that had happened in my life up to that point had created huge vacancies inside, an emptiness in my soul. He fills them.

Through our conversation I see a paradox: how God the Father has complete sovereignty, but he doesn't control us. He gives choice, freedom, to his children. He may control the aftermath of what we do, the results of our choices. He navigates, but we have agency. Some of my conversation with Jesus simply traces that sovereignty, the way my life has played out so far. Why it matters. What God sees. What he wants. What he is doing. What others thought to do for evil, God turns to good. Nothing is ignored, no wrong brushed aside. But his love transforms.

How deep, how attentive that love is. How encompassing. How careful. How complete. It astounds me. He tells me why my family members were the way they were and how that played out. And it all comes back to the same place: God knows. He has a purpose. He loves each of us intimately. Nothing in our lives is wasted. Our experiences, even the pain, matter. He sees them. He will use them for good. He isn't missing a thing.

It is okay.

I ask Jesus questions about me, about growing up, about how I could be like I was. I am so surprised that Jesus knows about it all. That he feels what I felt. That he gets it.

We talk about my junior year of high school, when a cheerleader asked me out on a date at halftime of a football game. I got so excited. At the end of the game, she told her boyfriend she was going to break up with him and was going on a date with me, orchestrating the whole deal to make him jealous. Well, it worked famously. He was big and beat the daylights out of me. Nobody stood up for me. I got in my car and drove home. I had been so alone. As I talk to Jesus about it, he tells me the real story: what was in her heart, what was in his heart, how I'd been gullible, available, and just happened to be there. It was a bad experience, but it wasn't a loss. He makes it formative. It was integrated into who I was.

Vignette after vignette of my life flashes through our conversation. Bad parts of my life. Good parts too—the moments sitting on a stool and listening to my grandfather, poking the fireplace, talking with him. Just being. The moments of reading the Bible with my dad. Of meeting Elaine so unexpectedly. Jesus had been there at those times too. Everything in my life appears in a different light.

———

Healing and reconciliation with my family came because of that conversation. It changed my relationship with my entire family. Even my relationship with Elaine was impacted positively.

That is what Jesus did for me as we ran our hands through the heads of the grass of That Place. My hurt, my family wounds, my pain—all of that was assuaged. Jesus made it okay. That conversation is why, years later, I was able to forgive my brother after his bipolar diagnosis and hear him say, "I'm sorry. I didn't know I was bipolar. I was horrible to you." And I could say, "Yes, you were, but that's history." Forgiveness was planted. The blood of Jesus covered it all. It was important and constructive and completely healing to hear Jesus talk about it all. He had seen it. He knew.

I was released. I was recognized.

All of it—the meaning, the closeness, the care, the overwhelming emotion of being inside pure joy, of being held yet free—this was the presence of Christ. He took all of my life before and all the richness of That Place and effortlessly focused it all on us, in the present, walking together. Our conversation. The moment.

I will never forget the communion of that walk. The union, emotionally and spiritually, with the Father. I saw Jesus as the ultimate bridge between the Creator of all things and humanity. He is the narrow gate. He is the bridge. Though I never saw the Father with my eyes while I was there, I had a sense of God as the caring, loving Father all around—not a God carrying a hammer to beat and punish us, as some think.

But the Bible's pretty clear—anyone who has looked on Jesus has seen the Father. And Jesus is the spitting image of his Dad. I saw the Son, so I saw God.

I had been raised orthodox Episcopalian, and now I was having a conversation with the risen Christ. I was in a place I loved beyond my ability to describe but was totally unprepared for. There was a sense of a whole new horizon of life and faith I never thought was available. I was processing this while I was still there, while we were still walking.

I didn't want to leave. And I didn't think I would ever have to.

———————

Jesus and I turn around as we walk. Back we go through the field, approaching the spot where I'd first set foot here. He still has his arm around my shoulder as we complete our big loop around the meadow. We stand beside the oak tree, his arm heavy and comforting on my shoulders.

But surprising me, he turns with a look almost of sorrow in his dark eyes. Almost an apology but not quite.

He abruptly finishes a sentence: "And you can't stay."

Immediately I'm back in the tunnel, weightless again, flying. Light is all around me, motion, movement—exactly the reverse experience that had brought me to That Place. What is happening?

The next thing I know, a nurse is leaning over me.

PART 2

THE PLACE BETWEEN

5

COMING BACK

I awoke in a dark room.

Monitors pulsed anxiously. Beeps and flashing lights came from all directions in the dimness. I was attached to nearly every medical machine you can imagine. Everything hurt. I winced as I desperately tried to fill my lungs, but I could gasp in only a fraction of the needed air. It felt as if an elephant was sitting on my chest. An oxygen tube was in my nose, though I wasn't on a ventilator.

I glanced down at my limbs. It looked as though someone had taken a baseball bat and beaten my entire body. I was bruised from head to toe. I later learned that nearly my entire intravascular system had been severely overloaded from extraordinarily high blood pressure. My blood had simply exited through the cell membranes intended to contain it.

A nurse leaned over me. She was pretty, blond, and blue-eyed and wearing a starched white uniform. A stark contrast to my dark surroundings, which I was about to learn was the intensive care isolation unit of the naval hospital.

"Welcome back!" she said so cheerily it was jarring. "We

thought we lost you back there." Then she disappeared, skittering off to get the doctors. Back there? I had no idea what "back there" was.

In an instant the room swarmed with people doing the uncomfortable tasks required of hospital staff: medical procedures, tests, poking, prodding. Pain stacked on pain as the doctors did all the things they do when somebody who is on life support and in a coma for five weeks wakes up.

Five weeks! After my collapse in the ER, I had been in intensive care isolation for five weeks! Unconscious and totally unresponsive.

I hadn't heard the ER nurse's response when, five weeks ago, she gave me the aminophylline and watched me crumple. She must have been terrified. I imagine her eyes going wide, her sudden gasp. Shouts then, as the crash cart came and doctors scrambled to save a dying sailor. To this day I still don't know the medical specifics of those moments, because I was not allowed access to my medical records. Whatever they did to keep my heart beating, they had to have done right away. Except for the heroic support of machines and medical staff, I would not be here today.

That—and the will of God.

————

When the doctors finished their initial flurry of activity and evaluation, they gradually started to disconnect me from all the machines. It felt really good as one by one the beeping instruments were wheeled out of my room.

But I could not get over the overwhelming sense that now I had to think to breathe. I could tell that something was very, very wrong with my lungs. I soon learned I had 60 percent damage in both lungs and a heart murmur. I had left this world with a cough. When I returned, nearly two-thirds of my lung capacity was simply gone. I was horribly emaciated as well—I had gone from 195 to 126 pounds. My own bones felt foreign under my skin.

This was all bad. I was reeling emotionally. But it wasn't the returning, as bad as it was, that tore at my heart. It was the leaving. When I first opened my eyes after returning through the weightless white tunnel, I was overcome with a profound sense of loss. I felt completely displaced. This wasn't where I was supposed to be! Everything in me screamed to return to That Place, to walk with Jesus again.

Over and over again in my mind I returned to my conversation with Jesus, seeking comfort. His love, his care, the overwhelming memory of being there remained perfectly fresh, emotionally fresh, even as I lay in that horrible hospital bed. It was excruciating to be away from it, but, paradoxically, the memory brought comfort.

Decades later when I told a friend about this, he compared the experience to taking a kid to Disneyland, letting him ride just one ride, and then tossing him back in the car without explanation. That, magnified a hundredfold, sounds about right. A profound sense of loss.

My five weeks of unconsciousness here had been like a blink in heaven—the time necessary for a meandering walk through a meadow with the Son of God. Time, I now realize, is profoundly different in heaven. Time as we know it is only on this side of reality.

To add insult to injury, I didn't return to a body in the same condition that I had left it. I was a shell of myself. There was pain, so much of it. Deep, physical, wrenching pain.

Part of the miracle of the whole situation is that my death had not become permanent. Under the extreme stress of my blood pressure alone, I should have had a heart attack or a stroke. Somehow, in God's sovereignty, I did not have a cranial bleed.

I had profound scarring in both of my lungs, making my every breath feel as if I were lying under an elephant. Beyond that always-stifled feeling, I felt alone and confused. Heaven had been so present, so rich and saturated with sensations. I had moved back into the world of bland. Again, I had no recognition of time. I didn't know how long I had been there. It was extremely disorienting.

Looking back, I realize it was a good thing Jesus had said in such a loving way, "And you can't stay." I never took it to mean "you're rejected" or "you won't ever come back." It was just "you can't stay." There was a timbre and love in his voice that made the loss a little better. His arm had been around me as he said it. I didn't like the result, but the way he said it was huge, lifesaving, life-infusing to me.

After waking up, I was in intensive care for two days, isolation for about a week, and then they moved me into a ward with an IV for fluids and antibiotics. I had a very hard time eating anything.

Over a two-week period I gradually moved from lying in bed to reclining, to sitting up, to swinging my legs out of bed. When I could do that without passing out, I got them to hook my IVs up to an IV pole, and I started to walk, although feebly. It felt as if I was learning to walk for the first time, and I had to remember to breathe.

Recovery was horribly painful. My body was working overtime, gradually metabolizing and reabsorbing the old, clotted blood from the bruising under my skin. This takes a long time and is painful. My bruises hurt. I had been immobile for so long, making circulation difficult, that my blood was clotting in my subcutaneous system. Yikes!

In the weeks after I was able to get up and move, I felt better. My slow shuffling around improved my circulation, though I didn't have the respiratory capacity to move much. My lungs were too scarred. What a far cry my hospital hobble was from the 5:45-minute mile I'd run in frozen clothes to qualify for SEAL training just a few months earlier. The sterile hallways seemed to stretch themselves in front of me as I made my way, step by step, down them, as if mocking the white tunnel I remembered so well.

My immune system, depleted not just from being comatose for five weeks but from months of swine flu before then, was far too trashed to fight off any infection. One day while I was in isolation, a nurse took one look at me and gasped.

"What?" I asked.

"You have the measles," she replied incredulously.

I looked at my skin. Yes, I surely did. Add it to the list. I wanted to laugh, but air was at a premium.

What next?

In life it's very good for all of us to come to the end of ourselves, to find the great "what next?"

There's a point where we do all that we can imagine to do, and it hasn't been enough. There's too much that lies beyond our control yet affects us intimately. We're stuck in the mud. Done. In the "what next?" we come to the end of ourselves and are forced to look past what we thought was the horizon and see what may be out there.

After I was moved into one of the wards, I may have been technically out of hospital isolation, but I was no less alone. The ward was empty. Bed after bed after bed, in an enormous room, stretched away on either side of me in sparse, even rows, typical of navy planning. Vacant beds all. Not a patient in any of them. I was the only person there. I felt as if I was back in the place I had lived in for so long—a world of vacancy, loneliness. What was I supposed to do? I had been inside pure joy, and I was back . . . here. In an empty, echoing room. Just me, alone again.

I lay by windows overlooking Lake Michigan and watched ships sail the bitter waters. I had enormous amounts of empty time in that bed. Since this was a military hospital, there was no television, no radio, no telephones. There was nothing to do. I didn't have anyone to talk to. It was nice when the nurses came by every four hours to check my vitals. But other than them, I saw no one.

I had a lot of time to think about my great experience in That Place. I felt disillusioned. The whole time I was in heaven I figured I'd be staying. A permanent resident. There was not a thought in my mind that I wasn't there to stay. None. I thought it was the end of life, what it was all about. And it certainly was great. It made everything I'd gone through in my life worthwhile.

But I sure wasn't there anymore, and there was a gnawing emptiness left by the perfect joy and peace I had felt there. Not only wasn't I there, but I wasn't even where I was when I'd enlisted. I had gone from a SEAL-worthy frame and the Annapolis acceptance to being here. Annapolis was long gone. A SEAL uniform was a joke, given my physical condition. I couldn't even walk up and down the hall briskly.

I didn't realize it at the time, but in this period of my life, the Father wanted me to have a wilderness experience—a season of spiritual wandering inside, when I had no idea what I was doing. And those weeks were certainly that.

Having heard that I'd come back, the navy started cranking its slow machinery, trying to catch up on the five weeks one of its sailors had been swept away by some unseen wave. Based on discrepancies and odd lapses in my naval records during that five-week period I was in the coma, I have the distinct impression they didn't think Steven R. Musick was going to wake up at all.

About a week after I went into the ward, a six-week bundle of mail arrived. Someone came into that great empty room with a bulging mailbag and dumped the accumulated stacks of letters onto my bed—all the mail that had sat uncollected at my quarters, my "A" school, and anywhere else that was part of my navy life. They'd just kept it until I woke up. The pile was easily the size of two basketballs.

I breathed in as the papers cascaded around me on the bed. Heavy and wonderful, I could smell Chantilly perfume. Elaine. A pang went through my heart, sweet and sorrowful.

Digging in, I noticed a letter from Annapolis. I tore the envelope open and began reading. They had heard about my hospitalization during the five weeks I was gone. They were revoking my qualifications for the Naval Academy based on my medical status. There went my plans, my path for education, and my officer's assignment. There went a whole future.

Sitting on my hospital bed after reading the letter from Annapolis, I tried to make peace with my situation. I still felt physically horrible. And I was absolutely emotionally crushed from having to leave the very presence of Jesus, a place of perfection, completeness, and total joy. Having Jesus tell me I couldn't stay was bad enough. But to return to a shell of the body I'd had before? To find out that all my plans, so neatly arranged, were popping like bubbles before my eyes? To be stuck again in this sack of skin, so limited, so far from heaven's green country that I knew now was my home? It was too much.

Along with my mail, they also brought all my stuff from my quarters, including my cassette tapes and player. They let me listen to music. I rested, playing all the songs Elaine and I had listened to as we fell in love—Barry Manilow, Carly Simon, James Taylor, and others. I still can't listen to Joni Mitchell without it having an emotional effect on me. As music will do, it takes me right back to that ward, to the strange feelings of returning, to finding out I was so different in every way from the man I had been only five weeks earlier.

As a kind of distraction, I simply began to put one foot in front of the other. I started doing laps around the ward as though it were a slow-motion racetrack. Beds, walkways, beds, then a half wall, beds, walkways, beds again. I was slowly pacing through all of it, over and over again. I did laps until I couldn't walk anymore.

Before the coma, I wrote letters to my family and Elaine all the time because phone calls were expensive back then. But my family hadn't heard anything from me for nearly six weeks. Little did they know that all my mail was piling up, unread and unreturned by the navy.

I found out later that during my coma the navy had sent my parents a three-by-five fill-in-the-blank card: "Your son has been _____." Several check-box options were on the back: (1) "Killed in action," (2) "Deemed missing in action," and (3) "Other _____." The third box was checked, and on the blank, someone had written the cryptic phrase "Transferred to Great Lakes Naval Hospital." It was the first thing my parents had heard from anyone. They were understandably confused and frightened. My father was furious, even calling our senator to demand answers about his son. None came.

In December I'd been on top of the world. Now, in late May,

I didn't even have my health. I drew in ragged breaths, having to remind myself each time to inhale. It felt as though I had lost everything. I felt fractured, devastated in soul and body.

I was at the end of myself, like a ship adrift on the cold waters I saw through my window. And life in the great "what next?" is like looking at Lake Michigan.

You can't see where it ends.

———————

I navigated the cool hallways of that hospital like a ghost of the sailor I had been, restricted to my ward since I was still under close medical observation.

My second week on the ward they let me roll my IV pole to the hospital's pay phones just off the main nurses' station. I called home. My mother was livid. It's laughable now, but her level of anger, undoubtedly from concern for me, was disconcerting.

"I've been in the hospital," I told her. "I couldn't call until right now. I just want to let you know I'm okay. Will you call Elaine?"

I talked to my dad, who was overjoyed simply to know I was alive. He told me about getting the cryptic postcard—the navy's noncommittal "information" about my situation now made sense—and calling their senator.

After we hung up, and with me still in my patient's garb, I wheeled my IV pole to the nurses' station.

"The chapel's still on the second floor, right?" I wheezed.

"Yes," the nurse said.

"I'm going there," I said.

"You . . . can't," she replied.

"I must," I said.

She tried to stop me. I was confined by orders, for my own good, after all. But I was being compelled to go to the chapel. I was adamant and finally convinced her. But because of my condition, she refused to let me go by myself. So she accompanied me on my trip downstairs.

Since it was about eight or nine at night, it was quiet in the hospital. The lights were dim, and the medical smell of the halls seemed as much a part of the place as the floor or the walls. We slowly entered the public elevator with the nurse shooting nervous glances, half-expecting to be caught the moment she stepped away from her station. We rode down to the second floor and then slowly navigated the hall to the chapel. It was the farthest I'd walked since I woke up.

I walked up the carpeted aisle and sat down painfully in the first pew. I looked up.

What am I going to do now? I asked God.

He didn't say anything.

I struggled deeply. Over and over again in our conversation in That Place, Jesus had pointed to moments in my life, assured me of his presence even in the bad times, and said everything was okay.

Is this okay, now? The question burned inside me. *Because I don't feel you now. Frankly I feel a whole lot of the other guy. Is this okay?*

My questions grew and deepened. This was a prayer straight from the heart, a heart in turmoil. A heart so confused.

What in the world is happening? Really, God? This is what happens to me?

The contrast between walking in That Place of perfect and pure joy and being back here in a wretched, wrecked, disabled body was too much. It felt horrific to a twenty-year-old. How could God do this?

As I sat for a while, I began to feel a little better in my heart, but there were no answers. I was alive and here, but there were no answers. That's all there was to say.

My breathing was strained, certainly, and that was awful, but this struggle felt as if my very heart was being compressed. Inside I felt tight and wounded at the same time. The last words Jesus said to me still rang in my mind: *And you can't stay.* What I needed to hear was comfort from the Father. I felt that he wasn't giving it. He was just . . . silent.

The nurse, knowing I was supposed to be restricted to the ward, was scared to death at breaking orders by sitting with me in that little chapel. She was fidgeting and obviously anxious. I could feel her nervousness growing, so I tried to reassure her of our trek's importance.

"I have to be here," I said.

I can't tell you how long we were in the chapel, but as the minutes ticked by, she got more and more skittish. I could almost hear her thoughts: *If the lieutenant commander walks in here, I*

*could be disciplined at captain's mast, lose a couple stripes off this
uniform!*

So, though I could have stayed indefinitely in that quiet place,
we left. She escorted me back to my ward, obviously relieved to be
returning, and put me back to bed.

"You've had a big day," she said.

She had no idea.

———

Days and nights came and went as May ripened into June. The
water outside the hospital looked warmer. I slowly recovered scraps
of my health, but it took weeks for my extremities to clear from
the bruising and clotted blood. Gradually my arms stopped hurting. Eventually it was no longer painful to walk. *That* was really
good.

I had to figure out how to operate with about a third of my
lung capacity, managing my airflow carefully, which is not an easy
task to master. I also had to learn to adjust to a heavy rotating
protocol of medications. They gave me meds to keep my airways
open, meds to keep fluids out of places they shouldn't be, meds to
keep my blood pressure at a reasonable level. There were meds to
keep other meds in check, meds to combat the nasty side effects of
still more meds, scattered piles of meds for everything, all rotating
in shaky bottles like a pill-colored merry-go-round.

But I got better, comparatively. Eventually the hospital felt I
was strong enough to go home on convalescent leave. By the time

I left, I had improved a good deal. I had hope. I didn't think I'd be sick for long. More important, neither did my doctors. "Turn this guy loose and send him home," they said. Chicken soup and Colorado air was the prescription.

They thought I'd gradually get better. They were so wrong.

I had awakened from my five-week (as earth counts time) coma on May 12. I went home on medical leave on June 11, having regained only 9 pounds of the 69 I had lost during that month. Weighing just 135 pounds, I looked like a prisoner of war when I returned to Colorado. When I hobbled off the airplane at Stapleton International Airport and locked eyes with my mother, she fainted.

I spent two weeks at home in Denver. Being with Elaine during that time was regenerative. There's nothing like being back in the arms of the love of your life after such a long period of separation and loneliness. It was extremely comforting to be reunited with her, incredible to experience how much she was there for me. She was even more supportive than she had been before—and this at a time in my life when many women would have looked at me and left, thinking they hadn't signed up for a relationship with a man as sick as I was.

I had been prepared for rejection, for Elaine to say my lingering condition was too much for her. After all, she'd fallen in love with a healthy man, and now his shell was coming back to her, hollow-eyed from a naval hospital, 60 pounds lighter, and wheezing for breath. I was emotionally prepared for her to go.

That convalescent leave was exactly what I needed. It was restorative and encouraging. It offered a glimmer of hope in a world of darkness. Getting out of Chicago's early summer into the mile-high beauty of Denver was healing in itself. I rested and ate. My mother made chicken soup and all my favorite foods. Just doing normal things like driving a car felt so good.

————————

My leave wasn't long enough, but I had to go back to Great Lakes for evaluation. After the ordeal in the hospital, all bets were off as to my future in the navy. I didn't know what to expect. They transferred me to medical holding while they did a medical board to evaluate my condition. In light of the severe and permanent damage to my lungs as a result of the swine flu vaccination and the subsequent allergic reaction, their review found me no longer fit for military service of any kind. I was labeled "disabled."

Uncle Sam didn't want me anymore, and that finger he pointed in the posters now directed me away from the service. The navy gave me an honorable discharge as a disabled veteran, which qualified me for GI benefits and meant I could go to college. I was released as soon as they completed the paperwork. As part of my discharge, I had to sign a release of liability, stating I wouldn't sue them.

I was young and just wanted to be done with it, to start over again. I genuinely thought that I was on the road to recovery and that I would get better. So I signed whatever they put in front of me. All I wanted was to start something new.

And just like that, the reluctant volunteer was a civilian again.

6

THE INNER STRUGGLE

After my discharge in August, I packed my belongings and moved back to Denver.

Elaine and I resumed our relationship, with marriage in our sights. She was accepted into physical therapy school, and I went to the school of business. Months crept by. The GI Bill education benefits, combined with my disability pension, were insufficient to cover my bills.

I spent four months in 1976, August to November, looking for work. But no one would hire me. You can imagine my résumé: twenty years old, little work experience, and a disabled vet. To top it off, I was sick when I interviewed. Even to a sympathetic potential employer, the wheezing kid in the ill-fitting suit was obviously unhealthy. I was still taking a hazy cocktail of strong medications to manage my symptoms—not a good setup to impress potential bosses.

So at twenty, out of necessity I started my own business—a financial advisory practice—even though I had yet to complete my degree. I had always been good with money, and I loved people.

This business seemed to bring the two together. It was worth a shot, I thought. I was just trying to glue my life back together.

Meanwhile, Elaine completed her program, graduated, and started her career in the fall of 1977. That same year my beloved grandfather died. He left me several items, including his threadbare and wonderful chair. I have it to this day. When I sit in it, I can almost smell the hand-rolled cigarettes Grandpa Mark used to make with Half and Half tobacco from a red-and-green foil pouch. I remember the smell of the stiff coffee in his mug on the end table in the morning and his Old Spice aftershave on his always-clean-shaven face. It's as if he never left.

All those mornings and evenings when I was a boy, Grandpa would sit and talk with me. He brought peace and wisdom. Gradually, as I searched for answers to my situation, the answer to a question I hadn't asked dawned on me. God wants a relationship with me much like the one I enjoyed with my grandpa.

As 1978 rolled around, I was busy working, studying, and romancing Elaine. We were married on April 15 by Father Kempsel in a little chapel on the University of Denver campus. (Tax day, so I will never forget my anniversary!) I will forever think back on that beautiful little ceremony as a miracle.

She actually married me. Wow!

———

There were many doubts and uncertainties during those years, but I never for a moment thought my great experience of heaven was all in my head. Not a chance. The hyper-reality of that experience seemed to have a residual effect on my memory of That Place. I hugely struggled—physically, emotionally, and spiritually—for years after my discharge from the navy, but never for a moment did I doubt the reality of what I had experienced on the other side of that white tunnel.

Part of that was simply the contrast I experienced between That Place and this one. That had not been a dream. It was not a hallucination. The vividness and strange otherness, yet the familiarity and lingering spiritual and emotional effects of it all, left not even a shred of doubt as to its reality. Unlike the memory of a dream or a typical experience, the clarity and details of my time in That Place have not faded.

But I had lots of questions. A great experience had happened, but I had no idea what to do with it. No idea how to understand it.

What am I going to do now? I wrestled with that question repeatedly. Life and faith could not be the same after such an experience. But it was complex. No voice from heaven interpreted my life for me or dispelled the difficulties of my situation. I felt I was on my own as to how to process it all.

And until I could make some sense of what had happened to me, I wasn't going to talk about it. I knew that opening up about such a deep and powerful secret would provoke questions that I couldn't answer, questions that would be very hard to wrestle with, even with close friends. Even with Elaine. Besides, I felt a longing to return always pulling at my heart. How can you tell someone you love that you'd rather be somewhere else? Even if it is heaven? How can you explain that the desire to be in the

presence of Jesus is so intense it hurts? How could people understand if they hadn't experienced it too? I felt like a fool.

I didn't have a large enough context yet for what had happened to me. I felt very alone in what I had seen, what I had heard.
In addition to that, it was such a deeply felt experience that I didn't
know how to share it, even with those closest to me.

I had to make sense of it for myself. It was good that I wan-
dered alone during this time. I had some growing to do. And that
had to happen on my own.

————

Of the questions that haunted me, the pressing one was, what do
I do now? I assumed I had to figure out on my own what to do in
light of my great experience since I couldn't yet share it with anyone. I needed to understand it. It was like a strain of music that
hadn't found resolution. It haunted me, playing over and over
again in my mind.

Those years became a classroom. I had heard Bible stories as
an orthodox Episcopalian, but we didn't really study the Bible. I
knew who Jesus was. I was saved. All of that. But I hadn't been
saturated in the Word in a way that could truly shape me, change
me. For the first time I began to dig into the Bible for myself. But
my mind longed for other books to help me understand the Bible
so I could study and research God's Word. For the first time I was
introduced to commentaries and other deeper Bible-study resources that sharpened my understanding and broadened my perspective on my faith.

During all that study one of the most powerful moments of my life occurred as I was standing in line at a Christian bookstore. I was buying a stack of the latest and greatest. And I heard a still, small voice inside say, *When are you going to read my book?* I put the top-ten best sellers back on the shelf, walked over to a rack of assorted Bibles, and picked out a study Bible. It was a huge moment for me. There was life to be found in Scripture. I was compelled to look for answers, to try to figure out why in the world I was still here.

Time passed, and I turned many pages of that book. I learned and looked and researched. I grew in my knowledge and love of God and his Word. I found powerful, compelling echoes of various parts of my story while reading the accounts of some of my childhood Bible heroes. But answers? During those long years, I didn't find any clear answers to my situation.

For a while I thought about the guidance system God had given the Israelites in the desert: a pillar of cloud by day and a fire by night to lead them through the wilderness in which they had been doomed to wander. I wished for such a clear guidance system for myself. Why didn't God give me one? Eventually that little inner voice spoke: *It's on your lap.* The Bible. Oh! *They didn't have the book; you have the book.*

I became disciplined in my Bible reading, patterning the man I most respected in that area—my grandfather. I built a special room, just as he had. I dedicated a place in the house for rest and quiet and being. For spending time with the Father.

In all of this, I wanted to understand God. I had shared a

huge experience with him, but I didn't really know him yet. This was the relationship that I needed to cultivate, that he longed for me to cultivate. I didn't really consider that God wanted to change the way I was for my good.

I read the full Bible five times, very slowly, the way my grandfather did. In a familiar chair. With a journal. Though I didn't understand who the Holy Spirit was at the time, I see now that he was helping me to read, guiding me into truth, encouraging me to keep pressing into the Word of God. My time in Scripture became a dogged pursuit of what my experience had meant, of trying to answer the question deep inside me: How do I need to live my life in light of that experience?

I read the Bible and tried to understand it as best I could. Virtually every day I spent time in God's Word, reading, highlighting, and journaling my thoughts and feelings. As months and years passed, my reading shifted and became more and more relational. Rather than simply an intellectual exercise or a search to make sense of a spiritual puzzle, my reading became a way of knowing God, of knowing the same Jesus who had pulled me close as we walked beneath the oak tree and had said, "Walk with me."

I sensed that when I missed a morning of spending time in the Bible, the Father missed it too. Not in a condemning way, but a genuine, heartfelt way. *I missed you this morning.* That in itself was a tremendous encouragement to show up every morning for my time in his Word.

I came to understand that everything in the Bible is true—ironclad truth—and I should read it as such. This is a different, deeper sentiment than the phrase I'd occasionally heard quickly rattled off: "The Bible says it, I believe it, and that settles it." It didn't get rid of the need to be thoughtful and skillful in how I interpreted it. In fact, I realized that interpretations of the Bible and its stories were all over the map. Neither could I easily dismiss the many passages that are difficult. It just meant that the Bible was—is—true. And that truth began to shape me.

I realized the Bible is the living Word. Parts of it apply differently at different times, in different cultures, in different contexts. But the fundamental truth, the truth that began to reshape my life of faith, is that everything in the Bible is deeply right. I was learning to trust it. I was learning to believe it. Among its many functions, the Bible is a tool, specifically a hone to sharpen other tools (like me). I was being sharpened.

All these thoughts and feelings and activities spun in my mind as if in a blender—whirling and processing and grinding. From his heavenly viewpoint God knew I needed to know him better, but that would involve difficult lessons. Having the great experience was wonderful. But it was not a substitute for knowing God. I learned to know God during this time as an adult, not as a child.

It's not as if any of us graduate from learning about God with tassels on our mortarboards and the knowledge that we've learned all there is to know. He is much too big for that, both in the Bible and in our lives. Did I find answers? Sure. To resolve every question? Not at all.

A little bit of understanding came. I understood that my great experience was real, that it was purposeful. And a few moments of experience I couldn't shake made me think that God's heavenly presence isn't just in That Place but in this one too. I learned to deeply know the character of Christ.

The point of this time of searching was that I began to find something better than answers. I found more of God. I had a relationship with him, and that relationship grew.

And isn't that how it should be? The communion between God and us should develop, deepen. We should change. We should be changed. When we grow in that way, the Father smiles. He is contented, satisfied, happy when we choose him again and again and again in how we live our lives.

———————

During those years there was a growing interest in near-death experiences and literature about them. I knew such books were being written, but I didn't have any desire to investigate them. I didn't read any other people's stories then, but much later I noticed some significant overlaps between my experience and others' experiences, such as the tunnel I'd gone through. But during that time of learning, I didn't hear about anyone else's similar experience. My own was too raw.

I was simply trying to work through it. To cope. There was no buffer zone, no clinical distance in trying to understand what had happened to me. I didn't want to talk about it. Everything about going to That Place and coming back was emotionally visceral to the point of being painful.

"You can't stay."

Ugh. I felt those words from Jesus in my heart, and they were heavy. I still felt the disorientation I'd awakened with in the ICU, though it gradually lessened. I still felt the heartbreak at leaving. I struggled deeply with the stark contrast between heaven and here. This world felt bland, and my body didn't work right.

My heart longed for the feelings of heaven.

———

In addition to the need to understand what had happened to me, I was working really hard to simply be normal. Altogether, I didn't really enjoy being here, though Elaine and our sons, who would soon be born, meant that family life certainly brought me joy and meaning.

It took a solid five years, but eventually my business got off the ground and began to be successful. I was good at my work and satisfied with it. There was a sense of being called to it, and it was deeper than just making money. My financial practice had a groundbreaking business model of full disclosure, no conflict of interest, and simply charging fees for services. It was highly relational and based on genuine love for my clients. This, in the late 1970s, was truly revolutionary in the field. Other financial advisors told me that doing business openly "that way" (in other words, on principles I considered to be fair and biblical and truly in the best interests of those who trusted me with their money) would never work. It was too radical.

What? Taking care of people wouldn't work in business?

Well, somehow it did. It was a fit, and for me it became a place where distinctions between sacred and secular didn't exist anymore. I became certified in my profession, and eventually I continued the college work that my lack of funds had interrupted.

One of the blessings of my position as a financial advisor was that I was in a perfect position to relate to people on an intimate level. I was fed emotionally on the career side, saw God's provision, and was able to help people at key moments of their lives. Heaven, of all things, was coming to earth through talking to people about money. I was beginning to rebuild my life little by little.

But I still had to think in order to breathe.

The process of how we breathe is pretty straightforward. We take air in and we breathe it out. But I couldn't take that for granted. The scar tissue and profound damage in my lungs limited my breathing to less than half of what it should have been. Only 40 percent of my lungs—the upper lobes—worked the way they were meant to. As a result, I couldn't really think about much else. Breathe in. Breathe out. The assumption had been that I would heal, that I'd get much better. That was wrong.

I did get better, especially compared to my critical condition in the hospital, but I was still profoundly compromised. Anything that required controlled respiration was virtually impossible. I couldn't sing, even to worship at church. The ability to hike at higher altitudes in the Colorado backcountry that I loved so much was gone. I could still fish—using my fly rod and tackle to work the streams and rivers was a haven—but I couldn't fish at a high altitude. Skiing was out of the question. The contrast between being very physically active and being significantly impaired was terrible.

————

Elaine and I had always wanted kids, and we were blessed with our first son, Jarrod, in 1983, when I was twenty-seven. Two years later Jarrod was beginning to lengthen his stride, walking and running faster than I could keep pace with. That same year our second son, Brett, was born. Two happy, beautiful boys. Both full of energy. And I was falling farther and farther behind them. What kind of father was I being to my sons?

As a kid growing up, I didn't get to play a lot. So when I became a dad, I was passionate about being able to play with my boys. But my lungs didn't let me do much. I felt terrible. They were progressing from crawling to walking to running, and much of what went on with a three-year-old I couldn't participate in. It killed me. What kind of father can't play with his boys?

I couldn't play soccer in the park with them. I could only watch my boys grow and literally walk away from me. I could root them on, but I couldn't participate.

I was desperate to be a good dad. Until they knew God as Father, all they really knew was me. *God, help me be your reflection,* I prayed. I wanted to be Christ in my own skin. I wanted them to know the Father because they had seen and experienced the Father in me. I didn't want their home life to be like mine was as I grew up. I wanted my sons to have a different experience.

During the years after my experience of heaven and disability, Elaine and I were welded together. That woman nursed me spiritually, mentally, and physically (as a physical therapist). She was always there, loving me in every way. She knew me. She cared for me.

Despite the love Elaine doled out selflessly, I felt incomplete. Undeserving sometimes. I was incapable of being the husband I so desperately wanted to be. So many women would have left. Not her. She was the biggest reason, by far, that I never carried out any darker thoughts, such as taking death into my own hands, which occasionally joined my longings for heaven.

Another reason I was motivated to press on was a shadowy sense of purpose from not being allowed to stay in heaven back in 1976. There had to be a reason I was still here. It felt like sin to indulge in the fantasy of suicide. Taking my life would be trying to assume control of my destiny instead of surrendering my will. It would be me taking over and disregarding the Father.

But I have to be honest. It was a constant struggle to keep going. I would have dark moments of longing when in my heart I just wanted to be home in heaven, no matter how I got there. Especially before our kids showed up, it was a battle to keep such thoughts at bay. A war sometimes. I loved Elaine with all my heart and soul, but I just didn't want to be here. Especially in a fractured body that wasn't getting better. I felt incarcerated in a sack of skin that didn't work very well. At the same time, I knew other veterans who were far worse off than I, and I was grateful for what I had. But still . . .

I have no doubt that had I committed suicide, I would have returned to heaven, to the God who loves me so deeply. I also have no doubt that our reunion would have drawn a *"Really? I mean, welcome back, but . . . really?"* from God. But that wresting of control from God's sovereignty felt as if it would have been a tremendous lack of faith, something that was so much less than what he has in mind for me, even though his full plan was invisible at the time.

But, oh, how I didn't want to be here.

Earth and heaven felt very far apart.

————

It was not unusual for me to miss several days of work every month. My immune system was still compromised. Whenever I was sick—even just catching a cold—it went straight to my lungs and laid me out flat. Getting sick strained what little functionality I had left, and it was very difficult to recover it. As anyone in a similar situation can understand, that is depressing. Especially for a man in his twenties. Especially for a young husband and a young dad.

Year after year I spent an inordinate amount of time trying to look normal. That attempt affected every part of life. I made careful choices about where I went, what I did, and with whom I did it, all based on thinking through the implications for my health and the appearance of my health. What would happen if I did this? What could happen if I did that instead?

This is life now, I thought. *I just have to figure it out.*

I'm an optimist, so I was in a cycle of constantly believing I would get better—and then being disappointed. The hope wore down as the years wore on. I did improve a bit; I gained some weight and strength. But the contrast between how I used to be and my present condition was stark. Almost as stark as the difference that always haunted me: the distance between That Place and this one.

The reality of always feeling short of breath is very difficult to understand if you've never experienced it. That awareness, that sense of panic only a breath away, never leaves you. The constant reminder of shortness led me to resignation. If this was the hand I'd been dealt, I'd play it. I didn't want to think of myself as a victim.

In my experience the longer people are disabled, the longer they think they're going to be disabled. My mind-set adapted and integrated into my challenges. I simply resigned myself to this was how I would continue to be. Since this is how life is going to be, I'll figure it out—that became my litany.

It never occurred to me the Father wanted something different than this Steve with only 40 percent of his lungs, the Steve with the questions burning inside.

And then the unthinkable happened. No, I didn't go back to heaven.

A bubble of heaven came to me.

7

BUBBLES OF HEAVEN

It was the spring of 1980, four years after my death experience. I was sitting in the back booth of a pancake restaurant, having an early-morning meeting with a client. I wore a pinstriped suit, power tie, and polished shoes, trying mightily to compensate for my young age and poor health. The client arrived right on time. He waved from the front of the restaurant when he saw me and then came and sat down.

As we talked, I noticed a man and his son walk into the restaurant and sit in a booth by the cash register. The man looked like a lumberjack, right down to a red-and-black-checkered coat. He shrugged off the coat and threw it into the booth. His son was a blond-haired, blue-eyed six-year-old and full of energy. I could see he was excited about having breakfast with his dad. The little boy refused a booster seat and simply sat on his haunches after he climbed into the booth.

I was in the middle of my presentation when our quiet conversation was interrupted. The lumberjack reached across the table and slapped his son so hard that he fell out of the booth. The restaurant fell silent.

Something went off inside me, no doubt triggered from the violence in my past. Someone had to do something. "Excuse me," I said, nodding to my client.

I walked over to the boy, who was lying on the carpet and crying. I picked him up carefully and held him. I was relieved to see he wasn't bleeding. I put the boy back on his side of the booth and slid in next to him. I leaned toward the lumberjack.

"Sir, you need to ask your son to forgive you for what you just did."

The lumberjack stared back at me. He must have been incredulous that this scrawny guy in a suit was challenging him.

"Who are you to tell me what to do?"

"I'm just a guy who doesn't allow things like I just saw go unchecked. Now I need you to ask your son to forgive you."

"And what if I don't?"

I turned to the cashier. "Call 911. Tell them to send a police car, an ambulance, and someone from social services for the boy."

I turned back to the lumberjack with an authority welling in my heart much greater than my own. "If you don't apologize to your son right now, I'm going to do to you what you just did to him."

"What gives you the right to stick your nose in my business?"

"What gives you the right to smack your son around? I know this wasn't the first time."

"It's the way my father raised me. Get outta here!"

(I've chosen to omit the profanity that laced his every sentence.)

I looked at him hard, feeling and remembering. "When you were your son's age, how did it feel to get smacked around?"

Those words cut his heart. The only sound in that restaurant was from the 911 operator whining through the old telephone receiver behind the counter. "What is the nature of your emergency? Hello? Hello?"

Tears filled his eyes.

"Tell the dispatcher it was a mistake," I told the cashier. "Everything's going to be okay."

I leaned toward the lumberjack. Time seemed to stand still for a moment. "Break this cycle of violence in your life. Right here. Right now. Ask your son to forgive you."

And he did.

For the first time since I'd walked with Jesus in That Place, I felt heaven surround me. Completely unexpected, I felt a depth of emotion, of restoration, of compassion, of rightness. I felt the pursuing joy, the active peace. It was a rightness of being that went beyond what was visible in the room and wasn't easily explainable in the unusual situation. There was an unseen connection with us in that Colorado breakfast joint, a connection that went straight to the fields of heaven. The only way I can describe it is that for a fleeting moment I felt something similar to what the presence of Jesus had been. It surprised and welcomed and overwhelmed me.

I wasn't alone in feeling its intensity. The feeling was like a bubble, fragile and beautiful, forming, swelling, expanding from that table for a good ten feet around us. It hit the cashier as she hung up the phone. She began to cry, her hand covering her quivering chin. Outside the limits of that space, people continued to slice pancakes and chew their bacon, ignoring now the awkward little social drama that had temporarily interrupted their breakfast.

In that moment our little haphazard group felt God's presence, his love, his welcome. It was like being inside pure joy, like being held yet free, like seeing life from a perspective more than human.

Leaving the dad and the boy, I walked back to my table and sat down, my whole soul taken aback yet feeling full for the first time in four years.

My client stared at me. "That is the most incredible thing I have ever seen. Where do you get that kind of courage?"

I didn't know what to say. Where? From some place, some person far beyond me. Or maybe not far beyond at all. Maybe much closer than I had thought.

More incredible things began to happen. I began to recognize these moments when I saw a flash of God's presence in a unique way. They felt like bubbles of a sort. Bubbles of heaven, I named them in my mind. Not like bubbles in an airy, fanciful sense, floating around aimlessly, but bubbles in a precious, fragile, irreplaceable sense. A truly otherworldly thing breaking into our reality. They come and they go, reminding us of the way things should be.

Each experience gave me a reminder, a taste of what heaven had felt like. Sometimes they were notable encounters or conversations, strange and deep in a good way. Sometimes they were pretty mundane. Some, but not all, were literally miraculous. What set them apart was a recurring emotional sense that I'd felt this before. I felt it there. In heaven. There was a quality and a depth to them, an inexplicable aspect I recognized as God's presence and care. The common thread in each of them was that it felt just like being back in heaven—the love, the joy, the clarity of meaning. The emotions were all there. Not with the same intensity, but with the same completeness. An echo maybe. The same sound but fainter. Farther away.

They stood out when they occurred, of course, coloring my life around them. They didn't happen a lot, but they happened enough to keep me going, to keep me looking for them. They happened just enough for me to remember that God is here, in this life too. *After all,* I thought, *I may be here on earth, but I'm still in the presence of God.*

One unforgettable bubble of heaven involved a client, Chuck. In the summer of 1980, Chuck and his wife, Bonnie, had just returned from a vacation in the Northwest. They were in their early fifties. It was time for their annual review, so we sat down and talked money. No problems or surprises. I expected to have a similar conversation the next year.

But in the fall, Chuck called. "I need to see you," he said. The reason was simple. In Chuck's vocational history, he looked like a tumbleweed, whisking and rolling from job to job to job. He never had a career, never really had a profession. Only strung-together jobs. The longest time he'd ever worked in one place was where he was working at the time. He was in sales; specifically, he was an estimator for a construction paving company. It was a good job, and this was the first time in his life he'd had a regular income. Knowing that history and the ominous nature of the telephone call, I thought, *This isn't good.*

"When and where should we meet?" I said. "You name it."

"Six o'clock, Tuesday," he replied. "Breakfast at the Apple Valley Inn."

When I showed up on Tuesday, he was in the corner booth. The Apple Valley Inn is one of those places where at six in the morning the cook, waitress, and cashier are all the same person. Good food, stiff coffee, no people. Just right on all counts. This conversation required space, grace, and confidentiality. And coffee.

Chuck was absolutely shell-shocked. He told me the story. When he went back to work after his vacation, he'd walked into the office to find a big computer workstation taking up his old desk. All his belongings were in a box with a sticky note on the front: "See the general manager when you get in."

What a way to get laid off. He was fifty-three years old and had been terminated by technology. A computer was his replacement. "And I don't even need to buy it health insurance!" guffawed the owner with a slap on Chuck's back as he was showing Chuck the door.

"Is there something you can do with our money to help us out?" Chuck asked. "Unemployment isn't cutting it. Job hunting is the hardest work I've ever done."

"Interviewing is hard," I sympathized, remembering my time as a disabled vet trying to find work.

"I'm not talking about interviewing. I'm talking about getting an interview," he said. "Look at my résumé. Look at where I am. I'm fifty-three years old. My work history is terrible. Nobody will even talk to me. I don't know the technology. I don't have the technical skills. What am I going to do? Isn't there anything you can do with our money?"

"Let me go back and look," I said hesitantly. "We'll see, but you just don't have enough to retire now. Next week let's meet here again to talk about it. Same time, same place."

A week later we sat back down at the Apple Valley Inn. Our coffee steamed. "Not only is your money situation not good," I sighed, "but it's worse than our conversation this summer. We'd been factoring in a pension from your job and years of income from the construction company."

We sat there for a minute. In an offhand way he said, "What do you think of Wal-Mart?" I started to give him the Wall Street rundown on the company—earnings per share, market, etc.

"That's not what I asked," Chuck said. "What do you think about Wal-Mart?"

"I don't know," I replied. "I guess I'm in their sporting-goods section once or twice a month. It's a big store."

"Ya know, they're building a Wal-Mart close to our house," he said. "They have signs everywhere, looking for people who want to work. I've never done retail, but I think I could get a job.

Although I'd lose about half of my friends if I even walk into that place. Union folks hate that company."

A week later he called me again. "Well, I took one of those jobs," he said. "I'm wearing one of those stupid blue vests. I stand at the front door and say hi to people. Doesn't pay much, but they give me health care, and it's a job."

Months passed and Chuck called again in the spring. "Apple Valley Inn, six o'clock, Tuesday," he said. I agreed to meet him, expecting the worst.

I got there before he did that Tuesday and took a seat in our booth. He came walking through the door in cowboy boots, new jeans, and a bolo tie. Obviously not working today. He bounced happily through the empty restaurant, came over to me, and slid into the booth.

For the next twenty-five minutes, I just sat there and listened to him tell me how much fun it is to work at Wal-Mart. He could hardly believe he was getting paid for it—hugging people, getting to know regular customers, helping them find what they need in the canyons of the big-box store. "I never would have thought it would be like this," he said, going on and on. "I love it."

I was so surprised. Then he said something that changed my life.

"You wanna know somethin'? I think God gave me that job. When no one else would hire me, God did. God gave me that job. That job is like heaven at work."

When he said "heaven at work," my eyes got misty and filled with tears. He was surprised by the depth of my response. He clearly didn't expect his financial advisor to cry over his job at Wal-Mart.

So I told him about my five weeks in That Place. About not being allowed to stay. About coming back, beginning to see heaven here on earth, closer than I'd been led to believe. Chuck was the first person I told about my experience.

He just smiled.

And for the next twenty years, he and I met early in the morning at out-of-the-way restaurants to swap Holy Spirit stories—moments we'd felt heaven breaking into our lives. We began to recognize flashes of the kingdom, bubbles of heaven. We talked about moving toward those flashes in order to see a bubble grow and expand. Right there, in his Wal-Mart, God worked in remarkable ways. God was in the places he went and in the people he met.

We shared story after story of bubbles, near bubbles, and might-have-been bubbles that we encountered. He spoke of being available for God as people walked into the retail store, of having moment after simple moment when heaven broke into the life of another person or into his life. He was available for God. Taking the time to be with people. Befriending friendless employees, embracing a hated manager. His coworkers didn't even know why they loved Chuck so much. They just loved to be around him.

We dialogued like two scientists in a secret laboratory. We hypothesized, compared, and rejoiced with each other. "Let me tell you what happened to me," one of us would start, and the stories would roll. Some were quiet. Some were frankly miraculous. All of them were glimpses of The Place I'd been, The Place I'd walked with Jesus, The Place my beating heart longed for.

I was so thankful for my friendship with Chuck. In him I had a person I could talk to, a person who could understand. Another person who could see the kingdom of heaven at work.

—————

The next big bubble came at the bedside of a dying client. Sometimes our firm is involved with health-care or end-of-life decisions. When Alice's family called, I knew what it meant. They told me that Alice was on life support. It was a miracle she had survived her stroke, but she had been in a coma for seven days. The time had come. I was named in the documents and knew the family well, so I was invited to be present for the final moments.

Her immediate family was in the ICU, along with their parish priest, who had come to administer the blessing of last rites. I stood and watched as the priest whispered.

"In the name of the Father and of the Son and of the Holy Ghost, I now remand you over to the heavenly hosts."

No one seemed to be listening. They removed the breathing tube.

We expected her to ascend to heaven. Instead, she coughed twice and woke up.

Shocked, the doctor blurted out a profanity.

"Be careful with those words, Doc." The priest put his hand on the physician's shoulder. "You're on holy ground."

Holy indeed. I knew immediately where Alice had been for

the last seven days. Her countenance said it all. She had been in That Place. God and Alice had our undivided attention. It was miraculous. A bubble of heaven expanded to fill the entire room. We felt it, but I'd guess only Alice and I knew the depth of what we were feeling. There was not a dry eye in the room.

A few days later Alice was back home, arranging time with each of her family members. She called and wanted to see me too. "Can you come right away? I don't know how much time I will have," she said. I wouldn't miss the opportunity to talk with her for anything! So we sat in her green room at the back of the house, where she tended all sorts of plants. She was one of those people who have a gift with green. Anything she planted grew.

She sat up straight on her short stool, gardening gloves in her lap. With a motherly twinkle in her eyes, she leaned toward me and said straight out, "Tell me about your time in heaven." I had never said anything to her about my experience. She just knew. There is a kindred spirit between those of us who have been to heaven but were not allowed to stay.

We sat and blended our experiences that afternoon. It was startling how similar some of our experiences were, but the differences were also surprising. I half expected another bubble of heaven to envelop us. None came. Nonetheless, I felt like a beloved son in her large family. She felt like a mother to me. Our time together was a perfectly timed event. God knew I needed another soul connection with another credible person with whom I could relate my deep experience.

By giving Alice the chance to come back from heaven, God

allowed her to spend personal, intimate time with each of her family members. Eight days later she slipped again through the thin veil of life and ascended to heaven once more. This time it was permanent. She had spoken the words she had been sent back to say, connecting with loved ones in specific, meaningful ways. Finishing this world well with her family.

———

Another bubble came in my office during the winter of 1983. Cindy, a sharp and confident physical therapist and mother, called me for an appointment right after work. Her husband, Roger, would not be joining us.

She still wore her bright uniform from the school where she worked. Its cheery style was in stark contrast to her demeanor. She looked shattered. Haggard. With her hands folded in her lap, she spoke in a quiet monotone. "Roger has found another woman and moved out. Since we are relatively new in town, I need to find a divorce lawyer." She paused briefly. "There. I said it."

My heart welled with emotion. How the Jesus of heaven cared for the vulnerable and alone! I began to feel a power and rightness that was far beyond me. Compassion—more than my own—flooded me. I leaned forward. "You'll need more than a lawyer, Cindy. You'll need an entire community. I'll help you build it."

The dam burst. I could see her relax as the welcome weight of a bubble of heaven settled on her. And I was feeling what she was feeling too—the focused love of God, a taste of what I remembered from years before as I was standing in the light and the tall grass of a field beyond this world.

What happened in that moment, what happened in the subsequent months and years and decades, was profound. With the words "I'll help you build it," a different relationship was inaugurated, a relationship that had some of the hallmarks of heaven—care, attentiveness, provision. My wife, now a physical therapist herself, joined Cindy's growing circle of support. We helped surround her with the right people to rebuild her life. We saw her and her girls throughout every week at church and in small group. The bubble of heaven we'd felt at the crisis moment held so many rich relationships inside it.

So, initially, I was a bit unsettled when she called a year later to say she wanted to see Elaine and me on a weekend for "advice of a nonfinancial nature." She came over to our home and told us she wanted to change jobs. She had studied medicine to work with people, to help them rehabilitate and find health. Her current job with the school district was a good one. It fit with raising her family and paid better than any clinical setting in town. But it didn't require the depth of her training. She sensed her skills eroding. She spoke softly about wanting to be involved much more in the restoration of lives, especially children's lives.

Elaine and I recognized her calling as a calling. What she longed for was something far more than just work. In the presence of such a critical and blessed moment, a bubble of heaven formed around Cindy—again—right there in our dining room. Tears came. Cindy became radiant. She glowed.

Cindy became a different woman in that moment. As a result of that crossroads, she took a job within a local hospital, treating children. She fell in love with her work. She resumed her calling in life as a healer of children rather than let her skills deteriorate in a school setting. She said later, "It was like finding heaven within my work." And I think she was more right in that phrase than she at first suspected.

Fast-forward to 2010. Cindy was by then the assistant head of her department in the hospital, working as a lead therapist. The hospital's HR department called her down to their office. She had accumulated enough points and was eligible to retire. "When would you like to start the paperwork?"

Cindy wrinkled her nose. "Do I have to retire right now?" she asked. "The truth is, I'm not ready to quit," she lamented as we later reviewed her finances.

"Cindy, you're done working for money," I said. "You can retire comfortably whenever you like. But that doesn't necessarily mean you're done."

As of this writing, Cindy still walks the mile and a half each way to and from the hospital where she works. She is still full of vitality, still beautiful. Her vocation continues to call to her as an assignment from God. She doesn't do what she does because it's her job. She is in the business of healing and loving kids.

The richness added to her life is impossible to measure in any meaningful way in the here and now. And it all started in one of those strange and beautiful bubbles of heaven.

———————

Our God is the God of the small things. While we are limited in our perspective, his is perfect. And what to us might first appear to be a simple social situation or a moment of human struggle or conflict, from his view might be a place where heaven itself intersects with life on earth.

What does that mean for our lives? It means some of the really simple stuff that occurs is huge, not to our eyes, but from a kingdom perspective. But it's dismissible here. We don't immediately feel its importance. Heaven on earth often allows us to walk past it without seeing it. That is the paradox of heaven as it slowly breaks into our lives on earth. You may have tasted it—a sample of heaven itself—more than once in your life. But did you recognize it for what it was? I'm not sure I would have if I had not experienced what I did on the other side of that white tunnel.

But during those often difficult years, those bubbles filled my soul like gas in a car traveling on a long highway—and always only enough to make it to the next filling station. I still ached for heaven, still ached to be the father and husband I longed to be. Still ached to return to the beautiful place I had so briefly seen.

And I still had to think every time I drew a shallow breath.

8

THE GREAT RETURN

From the time of our marriage until 1982, Elaine and I were semiprofessional "church shoppers." We searched hard for a congregation but couldn't find a spiritual home. It didn't help that we came from such diverse religious traditions. Orthodox Episcopalian suited me but not her. She was a Methodist, which did not resonate with me.

We shopped and shopped and finally settled on a small house church in the middle of Denver. We wanted somewhere to raise our children in the saving knowledge of Christ. This seemed like a fit. It was a far cry from Christ the King, but it was comfortable for Elaine. The Adams Street Fellowship was made up of twelve young families who met in an old garage with a potbelly stove to heat the place in the winter. We sang with a guitar and a cassette tape player, and we passed a hat for an offering to pay the leader who taught the Bible.

Soon our little growing church moved from the garage to a renovated space in the center of town. The little church was now 150 folks crammed into an old building. We affiliated with the Presbyterian denomination and became Central Denver

Presbyterian Fellowship. The denomination was so impressed with our growth, they asked the leader if he would move to San Diego and take on a much bigger fellowship there. He agreed, and Elaine and I never quite recovered from his absence.

So in 1984 we decided it was time to shop for a new church home. One of the people in our old congregation connected us to the Denver Vineyard, which at that time was meeting in an old liquor store. He said, "You gotta come check this out!"

It was a classic Vineyard experience—heavy on worship and very inviting. I had never experienced such a warm welcome or such focus on spending time together in the presence of God. They spoke and taught about the Holy Spirit as a living, breathing person, a person who could be known. God himself, in us. I loved it. It felt like home. For both Elaine and me, the Word came alive. The experience of church came alive.

Elaine, a gifted musician, loved the musical worship. Even though I couldn't sing because of my lungs, I loved it too. I loved just sitting in the room of voices and raised hands as songs of praise went up to God. We were there pretty much every time they opened the doors.

This was a church that prayed for miracles. And God gave them. Sunday after Sunday I sat and heard stories of people being healed, of God's power intersecting with their lives and changing them. It was interesting and powerful, yet I never really heard such things as if they were for me, as if I could experience such miracles myself. I didn't doubt their stories, but they just didn't fit into my experience of faith or church. It was weird—but in a good way. I didn't get it, but I liked it.

Despite hearing about the miracles of others and despite my experiences with sensing heaven quietly intersecting with life on earth, it never dawned on me to ask for healing for myself or even to ask for prayer for my condition. It seems a bit silly now, but that's how it was. I had accepted my situation as permanent. As the way I was supposed to be.

Frankly, it felt indulgent even to think about such focus being given to me, my problem, my suffering. After all, I didn't have any interest in going to church in order to get something from God. I believed you plugged into a community in order to give, not get. I didn't think that was how God worked. But I didn't understand the heart of God, the loving Father who wants to give good things to his children. I didn't understand how he wanted things to work.

We had been in this new church for about two years. This was about ten years after my death and return to a broken body. I had again become very good at hiding in plain sight, at coping. I masked my disability well. I don't think anyone else at church knew the severity of my condition. I never ran, played basketball with the men, or sang, but I was still involved and engaged. Honestly, I just wanted to look like a normal thirty-year-old. I didn't want anyone else to know what was going on inside me.

I sat in church and observed God moving around me, yet I struggled internally with my own questions. I needed to wake up to the reality that the Father had a different plan for me than isolation and continued confusion. He even had a different plan than my continued disability.

I'm not willing to make this a doctrine or to say that healing is some kind of automatic guarantee for Christians. We know it's not—at least not on this side of heaven. God doesn't work that way. His perspective is too different, and it would be unthinkable for it to always line up with ours. But I am willing to say that we who long for healing, including the healing of our bodies, don't have to hide. God wants us to be healthy in every way. He has provided for that ultimately, and sometimes he allows the great future healing of everything to trickle through to today. To you. To me. We need to leave room in our souls for the alternate reality, God's reality, which may feel surreal compared to our other experiences.

I don't always understand it, but I know it's true.

Why? Because it changed my life. Tangibly.

———

At this point my doctor's prognosis was that my debilitating lung disorder was permanent. Within a year after my discharge from the navy, my healing had plateaued and wasn't expected to improve. I was told to get used to prednisone, hydrochlorothiazide, and my general rotating cocktail of meds to try to keep fluid out and air going in and out of my lungs.

What might be minor to someone else could become very serious for me. Common colds had to be treated like pneumonia.

I required constant medication to bolster my perpetually depressed immune system. My impaired respiratory function impacted more than just my lungs. I now had an enlarged heart, by about 50 percent. This was my body's effort to try to pump more oxygen to compensate for my limited lung capacity. (On the bright side, I could say I was literally a big-hearted guy!) Medically, I was undergoing a siege with no end in sight.

When you live for a long time with a disability, you get a heightened awareness of your health and physical condition. I could detect my blood pressure rising and even the almost-imperceptible first hints of a coming sickness.

On a Sunday in June 1986, I felt myself getting sick. I could tell I was in trouble—coming down with what might have been only a nasty cold for someone in good condition, but it had the ability to lay my weakened body out flat for a while. Ugh! Not again.

By Monday I had fluid in my lungs. I didn't go into work. I was worse on Tuesday, so I stayed home and in bed. I knew I would be sick for a long time from this one.

By Wednesday I was thinking it was almost doctor time, but I held off, resisting yet another trip for medical care. I was coughing in colors, though. The bright mucus coming in quantity from my congested, shuddering lungs. I felt about at the end of myself. I was weak and exhausted, my trashed immune system already nearly on overload. I hated it all.

By noon on Thursday I found the strength to get out of bed and dress. "I'm going to church," I told Elaine, planning to attend the Thursday evening prayer meeting as a substitute for the Sunday service I'd missed that week.

Elaine was incredulous. "Are you kidding? You ought to be going to the hospital," she said.

But I felt an inner compulsion I couldn't quite explain and a growing desperation for my condition to change. For two years I'd listened to the messages at church about healing, watched the "Holy Spirit stuff" of healings take place around me. I didn't know what I was expecting, but I knew I needed to be there that night. I felt the same sense that had compelled me to seek out the chapel in the Great Lakes Regional Hospital. I just had to go.

I got in my car and made it to town. After shuffling into the building with the rest of the churchgoers, I chose a seat at the back, behind the sound booth. The music began.

The worship was so powerful that night. I don't remember the message at all, just a growing sense of God's presence, the knowledge that we were in a holy place. Then, in classic charismatic Christian tradition, they closed the service with altar calls. Not just calls for salvation or repentance, these were calls—specific calls—for healing.

Tom, the pastor, stood up front, calling out all orders of maladies. People were getting up and going forward for prayer. I sat and watched. This went on for a long time, and then they wrapped it up. Tom quit calling for people. He stepped away from the microphone to join the group ministering to those who had come forward. Then something stopped him. He turned back to the microphone and faced us.

"Wait a minute," he said. "Someone here has been dealing with a malady for years. A decade."

I listened.

"You've been sick all week. Sick sick. I think you have a respiratory thing."

Eyes wide, I gasped. No one in the church besides Elaine knew my history of sickness or disability. But I knew Tom was talking about me. I got to my feet. The compulsion I'd felt all day drew me and pulled me from the back of the building toward the front for prayer.

I didn't make it halfway down the aisle.

Randy Phillips, one of the associate pastors, came through the crowd with intention, looking straight at me. He reached out and put his hand on my chest. It felt like electricity went through my body.

I fell to the ground.

———

For the second time in my life, I am weightless, bodiless. I am flying through the same sparkling white tunnel I experienced ten years earlier, moving again at tremendous speed. It begins like an instant replay of the five weeks during which my body lay in the Great Lakes Naval Hospital.

Again, I am pushed out of the glittering tunnel and into precisely the same place I had stood before. The same oak tree stands there, the same forest. The rolling meadows rise into hills and then drop into a valley to my left. The same sights, smells, and sounds greet me. The tall grass bends and bows again under my fingers.

I am back in heaven!

Again I have all the feelings of heaven in their perfect completeness. I am held inside pure joy. Again my senses are saturated with the real-beyond-real of it all. Again there is the music and the lush color and the feeling. Again all is right. Again I am pursued to my very heart by God's explosive peace. Again I know I am in the place my soul was made for. Again all is so very good.

Again Jesus meets me with his strength and kindness. However, we don't stroll through the meadow this time. Instead, we simply sit near the oak tree's trunk in the shade of its broad branches. Jesus pulls me close, his arm again over my shoulder. We have another conversation.

This time he recounts all that has happened in the past ten years. His perspective again is perfect, insightful, meaningful. It makes sense of so much of my struggle.

But then he pauses. He looks at me. "Things will be different now," he says.

And with that, abruptly, I'm back in the tunnel. Weightless. Flying. Returning.

———

It was so fast.

I woke up on the floor of the Denver Vineyard church. The church was nearly empty by this time. Only three or four people were lingering after the service. The lights were shutting off. They had moved the chairs out of the room. My watch told me twenty minutes had passed since I had walked forward. They must have worked around me as I lay sprawled out. It seemed that such reactions were not out of their norm.

I lay there, trying to get my bearings, astonished that they had just left me on the ground. One particularly abrasive young man looked over at me. "Man!" he yelled. "God really busted you, buddy!"

Apparently God has a sense of humor.

But at the time I didn't notice the kid's rudeness. Didn't think yet about the miracle that had happened. Didn't focus on much of anything—except for one thing, one amazing thing.

For the first time in ten years, I had woken up and taken a full breath of air.

Things will be different now. Oh my!

The words rang in my head as I breathed and breathed and breathed.

———

I hadn't expected this. I hadn't known to expect anything. Other than a visceral compulsion, I can't tell you what drew me there that night. I had been willing to live my life the way it was. I had never thought it could be different. But now it was.

God really busted you, buddy! Yes, he did! I had never thought that God had a plan to bust me so roughly or put me back together so well. What a demonstration of the Father's care and love! He had heard my heart. Heard the longings for healing that I couldn't articulate. Heard my inner aching to be the father and husband and man I wanted to be. It was a gift. It was just a gift. It was going to change the trajectory of my life. Of that I was sure! Things would be different now.

I got in my car. The floodgates were opening. My faith felt real and renewed. My surprise overflowed. My mind was racing. My soul leaping. *I can't believe it! I can breathe!*

I gripped the steering wheel as I drove, my miraculously healed lungs drawing in air like a new carburetor. Those lungs began to pour out my brimming heart to the Father.

"Thank you! Thank you!" My gratitude was so intense it almost hurt.

"I want to know you more. I want a deeper relationship with you. I want you to show me what my life is for. Why I'm here."

And for a second time in my life, I had so many questions. What did this mean? What would my life be like now? What was God's purpose behind all this?

That ride home was life changing. I had a conversation with God. I was pretty used to sending up prayers, and though I knew God heard them, I almost felt as if they rattled around the ceiling somewhere. Suddenly it felt as if the communication loop was connected. As if God was speaking back to me. It felt like an extension of my face-to-face conversations with Jesus. Not with the same kind of clarity, but they were happening here—on earth!

The drive seemed to take forever. I was so excited to get home and tell Elaine everything.

We had a long conversation that night. I told her the whole story. Every detail. I told her everything for the first time: my death, my great experience, my inner struggle for meaning and for understanding why I was still here.

"That makes so much sense," she said. "It all connects. Why you came back from the navy such a different person! I always thought it was just your health, but . . ."

But heaven.

"Steve . . ."

"Yes, Elaine?"

"I'm overjoyed!"

It was the first time I had told anyone other than Chuck and Alice what had happened to me in 1976. Elaine now understood so much more about me. She was over-the-top thrilled about what had happened. We spoke for hours. Together we rejoiced and praised God for what he had done.

———

I went to my main physician, Dr. Jenkins, and told him the story of my healing.

"I went to a church service, doctor," I said, "and God healed my lungs."

"Really?" He was polite and professional, but a raised eyebrow and a gently condescending smile betrayed his understandable skepticism.

Until he got out his stethoscope and examined me. Then shock set in.

"Uh . . . Uh . . . ," he stammered. "I can't believe this, but . . ." He paused.

"But . . ." I asked.

"But your lungs sound clear and healthy. Living lung tissue sounds completely different from dead tissue. What I hear now sounds like that of a healthy thirty-year-old. Incredible! I'm going to take you off all your meds."

I was thrilled. My doctor, who'd cared for me as a disabled veteran with no prospect for further recovery, told me quite simply that I had been healed. The last words of Jesus to me echoed in my brain: *Things will be different now.*

"Gradually though," Dr. Jenkins quickly added, regarding my medication. "I don't want to do this cold turkey, but . . ."

"But . . ."

"You just don't need them anymore."

It was a gutsy call for him to make, given the severity of my history, but my symptoms were simply gone. God had literally fixed my body. He had removed the 60 percent scarring in my lungs that caused my disability.

Weaning me off the meds took about a month. Soon I went to the VA hospital and was reevaluated, because I wanted to give back my disability payment to the government. I didn't think I deserved it anymore. They agreed with Dr. Jenkins's diagnosis. Mysteriously, to them, I was perfectly healthy.

Although they confirmed I was no longer disabled, the attending doctor looked at me as if I were nuts to think about getting rid of a permanent financial award that I deserved. "If you have a problem with free money, there are all kinds of places you can give it," he said. He had a point, so I started putting my monthly disability check into a fund that helps release children from a life of poverty.

In the months after that, I got really healthy. I didn't get back to being the SEAL-worthy nineteen-year-old I had been before that fatal injection, but I sure felt good. A healthy thirty-year-old can play basketball again. I could wrestle with my kids in the grass. It was a gift, a pure gift from God, ushering in a new season in my life.

I embraced my life in the Holy Spirit in a new way after my healing. I understood I had been healed by the omnipresent Helper that Jesus had promised in the Gospels, and I embraced him as fully as I knew how in prayer, in study, in worship and praise. By inviting him more and more into my life to guide and influence everything I did, I got healthy spiritually as well as physically. My soul grew more than it ever had before. It was absolutely wonderful. Those are the kinds of seasons that you carry with you forever. Flourishing and rich. Right.

Things will be different.

Those words kept reverberating in my mind, echoing the good news.

I had no idea how very much they meant.

9

SEEING MORE OF HEAVEN ON EARTH

I had been healed. Healed!

Pastor Randy Phillips and I began playing basketball often, and I'm pretty good on the court.

"Man, you've been here for two years? How come you're not on our Vineyard team?" he asked.

"I'm just getting back into the game," I said as we ran up and down the court. "I've been out for a while."

As soon as a good opportunity arose, I told him the story of how I'd been healed that meaningful Thursday night. Healed! He was happy but not necessarily amazed. After all, God's healing power was all over that congregation, and moments like mine were always special but not infrequent. Well, I was still amazed. My life had changed drastically after that unexpected intervention from God.

After my healing I felt like a boy again. My two young sons brought out my inner child in a way I never knew was possible. After God gave me back my lungs, I had the health and the vitality to actually be a dad to my sons. And within two years our third son, Aaron, was born. Elaine joked, "I have four kids. I gave birth to three and I got one." It was true. I got to be a kid again, rough-housing and running and playing and jumping and wrestling with my boys. We played together a lot. I think that was the heart of the Father for someone who desperately wanted to be a good, fun, playful father. God gave that to me.

Because he had done this great thing, I wanted to pay him back. At the time, my theology was still largely one of compensation. So I tried to show how much it meant to me by being gener-ous. I gave money, volunteered, led small groups, and so on. It was all well intentioned, but my heart behind it was in error. I didn't understand yet that my healing was free. It was a free gift simply because my heavenly Father loved me. Just as I would give a gift to my sons for the joy of the giving, God gave me healing.

Still, I thought, even if largely unconsciously, that I had to retroactively earn that gift. Pay it back. I didn't yet understand God's heart of generosity. Many people—and I was one of them—equate God's work of healing us or giving to us with the prosperity gospel. That's a false notion that God exists to benefit us and give us what we want. That couldn't be further from the truth. But an opposite mistake of equal danger is to think that God is some kind of sour pragmatist who only gives something to you with divine strings attached.

My experience with the kingdom of heaven set in stone the genuine character of God. God does not exist for our appeasement. Nor does he have to find some excuse outside of pure love to give something good to us. He is a father. He loves to give things to his kids. Things we need. Things that make us joyful. Things that are good. Moments like this—when we are given something beyond and better than anything we expect—remind me of the second part, namely, it's beyond any expectations.

Still, whatever my heart was behind my actions, I entered a new life of ministry and involvement in the church. I began to lay hands on people in prayer myself, and God began to do amazing things. I began to be used by God's Spirit in a way and with a freedom I hadn't experienced before. Other than the few bubbles in the preceding ten years, I felt for the first time that God was using me in an undeniable way. And it felt so good.

More moments when I felt heaven here on earth began to pile up.

———

Elaine and I joined the team that prayed for people during church services. One Sunday a woman who was bent and curved from decades of scoliosis came forward at church for healing. I'm five foot eleven, and I was looking down on her as she walked up. We laid hands on her and prayed. A bubble of heaven erupted around us, powerful and healing.

Pop, pop, pop. Slowly deep spinal noises began and continued for about two minutes. When they ended, I was looking directly into her eyes. She stood straight and tall, her S-shaped back now erect. A beautiful auburn-haired woman. She cried and cried. God had healed her beyond her expectation. That moment was the first time in twenty years she had been pain-free. We thanked God for the miracle.

Another time the church decided to do something for Mother's Day. The ministry team stood at the front of the building, and all the unmarried or single moms—so often vulnerable and forgotten—came forward. We prayed for them. The single mom who walked up to Elaine and me was broke and broken. She had three kids and no food in the house. We laid hands on her, and God gave her a miraculous kind of relief in that moment. What the Bible calls the peace that passes understanding. That verse came out of our mouths. She knew peace for the first time in a long time.

When we finished praying, we asked what else she needed. "I can't feed my kids," she said. "I don't have anything."

"Yeah, you can," we said. "We have a food ministry here. We can help feed your family. What else do you need?"

That time became a Mother's Day miracle. All the practical things the kingdom of God is supposed to be about came into play for her. This, too, became a bubble of heaven. I felt renewed in a way so deep that I knew I had received more from God through that encounter than she had. I often wonder if those ladies from Christ the King Episcopal Church experienced a bubble of heaven as they brought food to our house when I was in grade school.

In that moment, so simple to appearances, I felt something profound and eternal and altogether good, something massively bigger than Elaine or me or the mom or our church was going on.

Now I see that instinct was right. Something huge was going on. A little piece of heaven was breaking into life on earth. It was so simple. So quiet. So good.

Today I have hundreds of simple (or not so simple) stories like this—moments when God worked in a way that felt just as it did when I was in the presence of Jesus in heaven. Hundreds. Each one is a flash of God's heart.

Or, as I call them, a bubble of heaven.

———

Between 1990 and 2011 I hadn't told a soul except for Alice and Chuck and Elaine about my first great experience of heaven. Although I had told many people about my miraculous healing, I hadn't felt comfortable sharing the story of my death, my visit to heaven, and my subsequent return to earth. I knew it sounded crazy. It sounded crazy even to me—and I lived it! But that all changed with the dream of being in my Subaru at that fateful intersection in 2011. That's when I felt God telling me I wasn't sharing the whole story he wanted me to tell. His words—*I could bring you back home anytime. I want you to get serious about telling your story*—still echo in my mind even now.

Shortly after my dream I called a family meeting. All three of my sons and their wife, fiancée, and girlfriend, respectively, gathered. We shared a meal, and I told my whole story. I wanted them to understand why I am the way I am. I was compelled to tell them. I had never spoken of this before to any of them. It just hadn't seemed appropriate before. I knew I now needed to tell my story to the public more widely, and I wanted their permission and blessing. All six of those souls, my three sons especially, encouraged me tremendously to follow that call.

I gradually told friends, my mentor, and close associates what I had experienced. Most of them encouraged me to take my story public, not just for me, but for others. Not just to impress somehow, but to encourage others to see heaven breaking into their lives. I was overjoyed that most of my community supported me in this mission to share.

Still, I had to get over some insecurities. The decision to make public such a personal experience and all the holy aftermath of it wasn't easy. I didn't want this story to be about me, and yet, because it's my story, it can't be about God without being about me too. Without personal vulnerability—not always easy for someone who was used to hiding for years—the story here is empty. I knew I had to tell my whole story because God wanted me to. And it was all grace, all because of him, all a gift. All a little taste of heaven.

———————

The classroom was over. I knew that a new season of my life with God was beginning. And I just wanted to give back to him by giving him to others—to you. He wanted me to share my story, the story you've been reading. But more important, he wants me to show you how you, too, can experience bubbles of heaven here on earth and how you can share them with others. Heaven is a lot closer than you think.

PART 3

FROM HEAVEN TO EARTH

10

THE INVITATION

Since my experience at that six-lane intersection close to our home, I have come to understand what telling my full story actually entails. It asks a great deal of me and a great deal of my readers and listeners. I'm honored you have joined me.

While the story of my life is powerful—I say that humbly since the credit for everything good in it goes to God—I believe the best is yet to come in this book. Don't get me wrong. I am passionate about my testimony of God's miraculous work in my life. But I honestly believe the story, the message I have told you thus far, is incomplete without the portion that is to come. My story is the what. Next is the why and the how. I also believe my future life on earth holds as much or more of heaven than my past does.

And what is really revolutionary is that I believe yours does too. God intends for all his people to experience and to encourage heaven to come to earth. He wants his presence and power to impact our everyday lives. He wants his love to characterize our lives. This third section of the book is dedicated to encouraging you to open the door to a new truth: how to experience the presence of a loving God over and over again and how to see heaven here on earth.

We need that desperately, don't we? In today's culture so-called normal life seems nothing like the way things should be. According to social researcher Brené Brown, ours is the most in-debt, addicted, medicated, and obese adult generation in American history.[1] How few of us live lives of freedom, lives of joy, lives of love, or lives of peace. How far that is from the heart of the Father for us.

We can feel so far from him, caught up in our sin and brokenness. We are so far from the lives God longs for us to have—lives close to Jesus, meaningful and whole. Honestly, take a moment right now. Does the world around you feel right? Or is life somehow just off, out of kilter, out of alignment?

Don't you want your life on earth to be an adventure in God's presence?

Guess what.

It can be.

I'm living proof.

———————

My 1980 pancake-restaurant encounter was the first time a manifestation of heaven on earth was so obvious and profound to me.

---

1. See Brené Brown, "The Power of Vulnerability: Subtitles and Transcript," TED: Ideas Worth Spreading, December 2010, www.ted.com/talks/brene_brown_on_vulnerability/transcript ?language=en (at 15:23).

What's more, other people were included in the bubble. At that point I realized there was something real here, and it felt like heaven. Pay attention.

That was the moment I began to understand something was going on around me that was deeper than I thought possible. It felt so close to where I had been. It startled me, frankly. *What's that all about?* I wondered.

After that experience in the diner, such moments came infrequently but perfectly paced, perfectly timed. There were plenty of wonderful and profound moments during those years, but only a few felt like heaven again, having an unmistakable sense of clarity, of purpose, of being held and guided by love and joy itself.

Things are going to be different. I think back to the words of Jesus in my second experience as we sat under the oak tree in That Place. Part of the way things were different was that I was looking for opportunities to engage others with the love of God's Spirit that I was experiencing so richly and freshly in my life.

In the years that have followed, I have learned to recognize how the kingdom of heaven breaks into our everyday realities. I see four basic principles that can identify what I call bubbles of heaven. Calling these experiences "bubbles" isn't perfect, but it's the best word I can find. Why? Because the sense of presence, of heaven on earth, is fragile. It begins small, grows and expands, and then seems to burst, leaving us different. These four principles are simple descriptors of God's profound reality. And just as they've been since the first time I recognized them for what they are, they are spiritual fuel for my heart.

This final section of the book illustrates these principles with stories and learned wisdom. It's my prayer they will help you see and encourage God's work in your life, experiencing with me the power of a life lived in heaven's light. These are the four principles (and the topics of the remaining chapters):

1. Bubbles of the kingdom of heaven are for anyone—even you.

2. Bubbles of the kingdom of heaven are closer than we think.

3. Bubbles of the kingdom of heaven will surprise us.

4. Bubbles of the kingdom of heaven are opportunities for God's love to meet earth's needs.

Read on, with a sense of prayer and a sense of invitation, to see how you can experience a taste of heaven in the here and now. This is real stuff. This is life. This is what we were made for.

KINGDOM OF HEAVEN BUBBLES ARE FOR ALL

E ven after my first encounter with the bubbles of heaven in the pancake restaurant, I didn't expect heaven to regularly break into my daily life. The very idea was still too new.

But as the years ticked by, my expectation to see them increased, along with the expectation that God was waiting to work in the lives of the needy to comfort, provide, heal, love, protect, cherish, and encourage. I wanted very much to be used, to taste heaven on earth again and again, and to help others taste it too. I began to ask God for perception and vision. *Father, make me aware,* I prayed. I slowly came to expect such situations, and then I began to feel when one was in the vicinity—a kind of sixth sense for the possibility of a bubble of heaven developing.

So in the years after my healing, I learned to be aware of what God was doing around me and to be conscious of his presence. I slowly grew in discernment and the ability to hear his voice. In our church I continued to grow in my involvement. The Vineyard's emphasis on ministry being a calling for all Christians and not just pastoral staff gave me opportunities to be spiritually available for others. I was constantly on the alert.

This world has extraordinary amounts of religion. We don't need more of it. It doesn't help the kingdom of God to expand. What we need are people who share relationship with the risen Christ, who live the loving life of the Holy Spirit in their contexts and their callings, who share the Father's heart with the world he aches for. Jesus said, "Thy kingdom come, Thy will be done on earth, as it is in heaven" (see Matthew 6:10).

I believe the bubbles of heaven involve time and geography (they're clearly places) where normal conditions are temporarily held in abeyance. Literally, the way things usually are gets pushed out as the kingdom of God enters the scene. Heaven breaks in to our day-to-day lives.

It seems as though they start with a flash of something God is longing to do. Then we engage by responding to what God is doing. I think the process is an intentional partnership. God includes us in the process of his work in the world, in the work of the kingdom of heaven on earth.

Do I believe the Father could act entirely on his own? Does he work separately from a partnership with his people? Absolutely. It would be arrogant to think anything else. But the glorious thing is that we are offered the opportunity to participate with him in his work. He lets us be a part of it. And when we participate, incredible things happen. The people involved have an experience that can be felt. It's palpable and undeniable. Believer or nonbeliever, those who are affected recognize that something different just happened. Universally, they are drawn to it. They love being there. They want more.

After all, being in heaven is like being inside pure joy. You get an echo of that when a bubble forms around you. I don't care where you come from or who you are, that echo will pull you in. It's contagious. It's memorable. It's what we were made for.

Every flash is an opportunity. I'm daily growing in my ability to see them, and I hope you can begin to see them around you too. It all starts with making ourselves aware of what God is doing and being available to join him.

———————

Once, after a church service, groups of us were standing around in what we half jokingly call the afterglow of a meeting. I saw a woman standing across from me in the room, speaking with her friend. This woman looked as if she was shining. She was more than radiant; she was iridescent with an unearthly light. *That's weird,* I thought. As I looked around, it didn't appear anyone else had noticed. But to me it was obvious that something was going on. I interpreted it as an invitation, and I decided to follow it. I walked over to introduce myself. When I was still five or six feet from her, my vision changed a bit. Inside the shining I saw all kinds of cuts and bruises—marks of abuse. I engaged her in conversation. When I thought it was appropriate, I gently put my hand on her arm. As soon as I did, information—specific things I never could have known on my own—came to me in waves. I received a supernatural insight into the specifics of her situation, and it was not good. She was in an abusive relationship. Clearly, undeniably abusive.

Prompted by God's Spirit, I began to share my history of physical abuse. I was gentle but confident. I spoke strongly, feeling deeply for her.

"What is going on in your relationship is not of God," I said. "The things being done to you? They are wrong. They are not allowed. They are not appropriate."

The woman was gripped by my words.

"And," I continued, "they are not your fault."

Her friend looked aghast. *How do you know?* her eyes asked.

As it turned out, the abused woman had told virtually no one besides her friend standing with her. *That's the word of the Lord,* I thought. But I didn't have the whole story yet. I assumed she was divorced. A single mom perhaps. I finished, really trying to love her in the situation, to encourage her and discover what she might need. Looking for an opportunity to help somehow, I finally said, "Tell me about your family."

She looked past me, into the hall, at her husband. The man who was abusing her.

"Well, there's Ted now," she said. She hollered, "Honey! This man has a word from God for you!"

I turned and looked at him. He was a *big* guy. A *very big* guy. *Uh-oh,* I thought. He's probably going to rip off my arms and beat me with them for talking to his wife!

He walked over, and I braced myself for a conflict.

And then a quiet miracle happened. When he was about five

or six feet from us, he entered the bubble of heaven that had begun to form. His countenance transformed. Before a word had even been said, conviction was written all over his face. With a boldness that could only have come from God's Spirit in that moment, I lovingly but sternly told him what I had told his wife.

He began to weep big tears of repentance. I knew right then that God was starting to work in this man's life.

Do I know what happened to this couple? No, I don't. I had never seen them before, and I've not seen them since. That's not unusual in my experience with bubbles of heaven.

I could share many stories like this where a visual cue from the Spirit is used to start something amazing, some little influence of God's love and righteousness here on earth. Where a little awareness and making myself available opened the door for the work of heaven.

I've noticed that the bubbles, while certainly present in church, are not limited to it. In fact, some of the most powerful bubbles have occurred outside of church, or at least what I had been trained to think of as church. It's easier to picture heaven coming to earth in a spiritual place like a church or a house of worship, but I've seen bubbles appear at the most ordinary, everyday places— supermarkets and diners, hospitals and office buildings.

One of the most beautiful examples of this I ever saw was at a place called Hope Ranch, near Wichita, Kansas. The reason this place highlights the power of emotional freedom so starkly is the darkness there that serves as a backdrop for the Father's light.

The women of Hope Ranch are all victims of human trafficking. Only just coming to the public's attention, the trafficking
of sex slaves in America is a dark, filthy industry. It's big business
trading in exploited bodies and destroyed lives.

Young women are kidnapped, drugged, and sold into the sex
trade as slaves to their owners, an insidious result of humanity's
most blatant carnal appetites. This kind of trafficking has become
pervasive, slithering in every large city in America and even in-
filtrating some smaller towns. It's very difficult to combat. The
enemy is sophisticated. The business is lucrative. And the conse-
quences are few for the proprietors who are apprehended.

Hope Ranch is fighting all of this, though. The ranch is a
haven for trafficked women, a place where tattered lives can be re-
built. A team of people—some professional, but mostly volunteers—has created a safe place for these women. And this place is
as close to heaven as you will find on earth. That's precisely why it
is so effective. Hope Ranch is a place of pure joy, security, and
peace for these women who want to be freed from the incarceration
of the drugs that kept them bound to their captors. The women are
hidden, in fact, from their former owners in order to heal, to begin
to come out of the shells that their trauma, dependency, and exploitation have created.

Over a ninety-day period, the women go through a detox
program with a local agency. Once clear of the drugs, they are
transferred four at a time to the ranch. Over a two-year period,
they are restored to health and vitality and are prepared to reenter
normal society.

Because of the violence and brutality of the criminals they've been delivered from, the process is much like the witness protection program. They become very different people. They get a brand-new start. They exchange their old life for a new one.

Walking onto the grounds of the ranch is like stepping straight into a bubble of heaven on earth. It's emotional, powerfully so. How could it not be? The process of healing for these women is raw.

Hope Ranch is a faith-based work supported by donations, public agencies, and law enforcement. And this public-private partnership actually works. Cathy, a married woman who was in midcareer, started the ranch.

Cathy responded when her calling called. She has two married children and three grandchildren, and she will instantly dig into her purse and pull out a smartphone chock-full of photos of her incredible kids and grandkids. But ask her to talk about the women caught up in human trafficking, and she comes apart. How can sex slaves rival—and in some cases exceed—the passion you have for your own family? Because heaven is at work in the here and now at Hope Ranch. God gave her his heart for women caught up in this horrible reality.

Cathy and her husband of thirty-one years successfully redefined their family. For them, blood, marriage, or law does not determine family. So they embrace these women as family. And as a result, these women experience a taste of heaven without dying. Why? Because the sheer power of heaven is the only way to be truly extracted from the clutches of their tormentors.

But it is not easy. Not at all. Healing hurts sometimes. It has to, in order to be real.

As we peel off our layers of self-defense, we become more vulnerable to pain. But the antidote to pain is not a narcotic that numbs us; it's a touch from God that heals us. It's organic. Natural. Not something we have to synthesize or manufacture. It's real. The Father works through the exact pain we are so afraid of in order to bring wholeness and restoration.

It's kind of a silly picture, but I really like the imagery of a butterfly. Instead of remaining in the cocoon—protected but dormant, encapsulated, immature—we need to be like the butterflies that emerge from them. This molting process makes us sensitive to the world around us. We're no longer safe and sealed inside the protective casing we make for ourselves. But now we are free, able to fly, to spread our wings, to be sensitive to the presence of the Father. Free to feel the sun.

When we encase ourselves in protective shells, we hold all our junk and baggage in there with us—our hurts, wounds, and bitterness. As we break through the layers that imprison us, we more easily deal with all that. And the process makes it easier for the Father to deal with our weaknesses and sins and easier for us to give them over to him and to begin the cleansing process. It's as if we let God turn our lives inside out so our hearts, far from being hidden away, drive our interactions with others.

Entire encyclopedias could be published to catalog the emotional baggage we carry with us and continue to inflict on ourselves. God wants to do away with all of it. When we volunteer to live this way, we give the Lord greater access to do just that. He takes away our burdens. He took mine away. Trust me, I know firsthand: there's a whole bunch of stuff we carry around that we just don't have to. We just don't. That's a very freeing process. It's like a breath of fresh air after being enclosed in a hot, stuffy room.

Cultural norms that hinder our honest, deep emotional expression ought to be done away with. When tears need to come, we should let them. When laughter bubbles up from a holy heart, keeping it down is not of God. It's healthy to feel and to express those feelings.

Most often, my early signal for a flash of heaven is compassion. When I'm close to someone and feel unusual compassion for him or her, I know there's a very strong possibility a bubble of heaven is forming. Initially, I believe it's a discipline to live this way, to live inverted. It takes willpower and a decision to remain open to God's leading, even if it's not comfortable. But over time you grow into it. It becomes the way you function.

Stereotypically, this is easier for women and harder for guys. But it's really important to get in touch with what's happening emotionally inside you. It's a way you can sense what God is doing around you. It's good to be sensitive. It means you're making yourself available for God to use you. When was the last time you were overwhelmed emotionally? Go back there. Revisit it in your mind, because maybe that was where you were closer than ever to a taste of heaven. Culturally, we don't want to go there. But I'm telling you to go there. And stay for a while. Think about it. Apply that to the next time. Live with an open heart, because the Father speaks through our emotions.

Time after time when a bubble of heaven has been near, I've noticed I feel some things more deeply than I should. And in that flash point, God has begun to work in situation after situation. It's powerful!

I think we can choose to practice this and grow into deeper and deeper levels of feeling for others. We look on so many things now with a sort of resigned indifference. It's powerlessness. I think that's the Enemy. The antithesis of that, the polar opposite, says, "Not on my watch." We must engage. We must feel and do something about it.

Jesus is moved with compassion when he sees anyone in need. He wept before. He feels something now. So should we. Love is the language of heaven. True, good, honest love. Love that cares and moves to redeem and reclaim pain and loss. Love that pulls others closer and then walks together with them. Christ is God the Father wrapping his arm around the broken. And on this earth, he does that through his people. But are we as eager to reach out as he is?

In a culture that highly values personal space, we're often disconnected from the power of simply, appropriately, and humbly closing the distance between others and ourselves. God uses touch and closeness to tremendous effect. It was one of the most powerful and lingering parts of my experience in heaven, and I recognize it when I sense a bubble forming. Imagine human contact and closeness without the fears, insecurities, and cultural mores that have accrued and attached themselves to our ideas about touch and physical distance. Remember how good it feels to be close to a safe, caring person—someone that you know wants nothing from you but only wants to give and cherish you as a valuable person. That is the sense of touch in these bubbles of heaven.

I'm very careful about touch. There are too many ways it can be misinterpreted. But there are times when the loving touch of the Father, transmitted through you or me, is exactly what one of his children needs in a given situation.

Learning to see and practice the flashes of heaven is partially the discipline of learning to live inverted. In many ways God's kingdom turns the ways of the world upside down. God's ways are full of paradoxes, and if we live in his way, we join him in those good tensions.

The economics of the kingdom of heaven are upside down: giving is better than getting, death can be life, life as the world sees it can be death, loss can be gain, gain can be loss. God's kingdom often flips the way we do little things upside down. In our culture we insulate ourselves in all kinds of ways. We cocoon. When the situation calls for it, God's volunteers need to be able to strip away the cultural things that keep people apart.

Many of us are not in touch with our emotions. Or maybe we are uncomfortable with them. Perhaps we have never thought how God might use our emotions in our lives or in the lives of others. It took time for me to change, for the emotional suppression I had learned when I was younger to diminish. As a result of having the great experience and continually experiencing bubbles of heaven, I've been emotionally changed forever. I no longer need to guard my emotions. The protective armor around my heart became unnecessary.

I'm not alone in this. All of us need to ask God to make us continually sensitive and emotionally available when opportunities to share and experience his love may be close to us. In fact, we all know the feeling—that gentle, uncomfortable prompting inside. It's like a pinching of our souls. Most of us try to ignore it. But we have no idea what we're missing if we do.

We just might be missing a taste of heaven itself.

We need to ask God to make us sensitive to circumstances and environments, to people and their needs. We need to ask him to help us be present—that foundational quality of heaven that is so difficult to attain in a world of distraction. We need to ask God to help us feel what others feel, to tune in to the emotional states of others just as he does.

As we learn to ask for these things, and as God gives them to us (usually slowly), we end up with a combination of qualities that I think look a lot like Jesus himself. If God gives them to us, we begin to bear the fruit of the Spirit—love, joy, peace, patience, kindness, goodness, gentleness, faithfulness, and self-control. We begin to walk with a quiet strength that is a little taste of how we will walk in heaven. Our perspectives will be broadened, our faith deepened, our hearts nourished.

This whole process of joining God in heaven's work is not something you can pick up and decide to do in your own power.

It's not like clothes—an identity you can put on or take off. Instead, seeing God at work and joining him nourishes you.

We can start every day by volunteering for service to God. As Christians, we need to snap to attention like sailors, salute the Father smartly, and say, "Count me in." It's the best thing we can do. When we say that, we're in for the ride of a lifetime. This is not an arrogant claim; I say it humbly. I want to encourage you simply to come along with God. Join with me as I try to follow heaven's lead here on earth. You can say no, but please don't. There's a richness available that we have barely begun to sense. And it's available to all of us.

12

KINGDOM OF HEAVEN BUBBLES ARE CLOSE

Early in his ministry, Jesus sent seventy-two followers throughout Judea to preach, heal, and do the things Jesus himself was doing (Luke 10:1–12). They were to heal and cast out demons and bring very practical tastes of the kingdom they preached about to their land. What was their message? "The kingdom of God has come near to you" (verse 9, ESV).

It's right here in the Bible! The kingdom of heaven is a lot closer than we've been led to believe. We need only to open the door to allow it in. And when we do that, life changes. The quality of our lives literally changes. My great experience changed me forever. Every time I take a breath without having to think about it, I receive a gift. To be disabled for ten years and then, all of a sudden, not to be. It's amazing! The kingdom of heaven has come near to me!

It's surely amazing, but the truth is, we're not talking about wild and crazy stuff here. This is how normal should be! There's just so much more to God's normal than we think.

How do we get to that? It's simple but not easy. We get there by being in a place where we recognize the kingdom is near and then opening the door. Not so we can go out, but so the kingdom can come in. Not to make the journey of faith simply about our getting to That Place, to heaven, but for the God of That Place to bring heaven right here.

Today.

What do you do with that? If the people in your circle of the world received a taste of heaven, what would life be like?

Would it change the way you relate to them?

Would it change the way you respond?

Would life be different?

Do you think your life could be different?

I know it can.

I believe my life today is at another crossroads, an inflection point. I have the overwhelming sense I'm beginning a season that will be different from the ones that went before. Different and really, really good. I now understand why I'm still here. I now understand why I couldn't stay in heaven. I now understand my healing after ten years of disability and why things are different.

Reviewing my life, I've reached the profound conclusion that the Lord could take me home at any time. *Pop!* In the time it takes to snap my fingers. I'm ready to go back again. Yes, Elaine and my boys would be very sad. It would not be easy for the people I'd leave behind, but I'd be a happy guy in the presence of Jesus again, looking at him face to face like any of us here look at a friend.

But I don't think that's in the cards. The reason I'm alive, the reason I'm still here, is simple. My purpose is to make my death *worth living for.*

I mourn what we're missing here on earth. I mourn for the things God offers us here that we somehow choose not to appropriate. I mourn the fullness we ignore, the love we don't recognize, the power and joy just waiting to be picked up by us. I would like to help everyone I can to receive a full measure of what's offered.

Why am I still here? I think it's simple. My purpose, my calling, for the rest of my days is to tell people the kingdom of heaven is closer than we think. It's not heaven to the full. But it's *close.* And it will do for now, until we ascend permanently or until Jesus returns to reign. Doesn't that sound like good news?

I do what I can to be close to God. But his presence is always pure grace. A gift. No one can make it happen.

It's like an old Vineyard expression that some people say George Eldon Ladd coined: the kingdom is "now and not yet." It's a paradox. Here but not fully here. Present but still coming. I see it all the time. In my world it's an echo of what I personally experienced in heaven. It's not the full thing, but it's the real thing. And for now it'll do.

It'll do.

I have a foot in each of two worlds. On the one hand, I'm ready and eager to go back to heaven at any moment. On the other hand, I'm here. I know God here. I serve Jesus here. Putting all my attention on the hereafter distracts from the mission today. It distracts from love today. In that sense, seeing heaven only as there, ironically, can keep us from experiencing it now.

I'm prepared to travel through that white tunnel again at any moment, to be embraced by Jesus again, and never to leave his side. But in terms of life on earth, well, I still have a retirement account. I understand it might not be God's will for me to leave here anytime soon. I can live in that tension for now.

Heavenly living on earth looks like living out heaven on earth. That makes this life—for all its pain and blandness (compared to life in That Place)—heavenly. It is freedom in Christ, not an imprisonment. "To live is Christ," Paul said, "and to die is gain" (Philippians 1:21, ESV).

Doesn't that sound like something God would do?

The most important thing for all of us lost ones on earth is that we should be found by the God who is searching for us. Deep down we want to be found by Christ. We want Jesus to put his arm around us. To see us. To speak to us. We want to be found in him. Nothing richer is available to humanity. Everything else pales in comparison. Everyone who has been born is on a level playing field, all riches and privileges stripped away, with the same lostness and the same hope of being found again.

The principles that shape heavenly living on earth are all the same. But how these principles are lived out practically looks a little different for everyone. I may have an idea of what the practical application of vocational transformation in your church may look like, but my opinion's just an opinion. It's your life, and God will guide you in how to live it out best.

In all of this, we are simply trying to see what the Father is already doing. There's no recipe for this because there's no recipe for relationship. We work to align our hearts with the heart of God, our emotions with his emotions, our resources with his, our knowledge with his. We are simply volunteering to be his agents in a world that needs his influence so much. In simple, practical, tangible ways, we are volunteering to help do the true work of the kingdom through Jesus. To bring heaven to our world.

I think we walk past tremendous opportunities without recognizing them. Part of the problem is that we're inclined to think of sharp distinctions between the spiritual and physical realms. Those distinctions feel major to us, but they're not part of God's experience. He transcends them even as he works within them.

I think we have these kinds of opportunities all the time. But we miss them or dismiss them. Our cultural norms get in the way perhaps, or we simply lack the expectation that God actually wants to work through us. We end up living a diluted version of Christianity. We're like diluted wine—still wine, but thin.

Part of the power of this is the Father's whisper to us: Return. Return to the original. On the road to Emmaus, the risen Christ encountered two disciples, and they failed to recognize him until he chose to reveal himself (Luke 24:13–32). We should all have that kind of Emmaus road experience. It should happen a lot, spiritually speaking. So why doesn't it? Why don't we learn to see Jesus in the places we aren't expecting to find him?

One reason is that we're held back by the norms of our culture. For example, the cultural norm of privacy gets in the way. It feels safe to stay in our own stuff and let others stay in theirs. We feel awkward about invading the space of another person. And sometimes others feel awkward when we invade their space—at least at first.

But there are times it's okay to step into places where a door is opening, where there's opportunity. It's what's needed. It's okay to sensitively violate norms if the intent is to love the other person.

Our addiction to material goods is another huge hindrance. The national mantra to get all we can, can all we get, and then sit on the can is our cultural norm. We are a collective of misers. We spend our lives accumulating stuff—the exact opposite of God's will. Meditate for a moment on this powerful scripture: "God is able to bless you abundantly, so that in all things at all times, having all that you need, you will abound in every good work" (2 Corinthians 9:8, NIV). Our surplus should be for alleviating the deficits of others. We need to notice and readily respond to circumstances with whatever resources God has entrusted to our care. Following Christ leads us to be generous.

Poverty in God's kingdom is not a lack of things; it's the grasping for them. Real poverty is tightly holding on to what you're supposed to give away. What do you think the Father would do if you actually lived this way, followed his Son in this way? And did so with earnest intentionality? What would you do? What would life be like?

Exactly what does living in the light of heaven look like in your world? How would God bring the bubbles of heaven into your life? I can't tell you exactly, though I might have ideas if we were to meet over coffee. This is a journey all of us must walk for ourselves, following the common principles that God works by to live out our faith on a practical level. To live out heaven on earth in a practical way. How do you want to do this? What do you want to see happen? How will you recognize and join the Father's work today?

My best advice if you want to live this way is that you should intentionally invite the Father into your life. It will forever be different if you do. He will take whatever time you give him, occupy whatever space you allow him, and accept your invitation every time.

Invite him into all aspects of your life, waking and sleeping, thinking and dreaming. Follow where he leads.

Be open and willing to consider the many ways God can speak, including dreams, feelings, and Bible reading. The walk of faith is a life, not a formula. Over time you will reach a point where you begin to feel what the Father feels. You'll see circumstances that pierce you—joy, suffering, sorrow, brokenness, isolation.

Not all experiences of heaven on earth are miraculous or supernatural. Sometimes they are ordinary—or so they might seem. But the feelings that come with them—the sensations within a bubble—are every bit as powerful.

Pause for a minute. You've heard my story. I'm the kid used to hiding, to being vanilla, to blending in. Put yourself in my shoes for a minute. I'm an introvert by temperament. Besides that, most of the major forces that shaped my life—from my early family life to entering the first ten years of adulthood as a disabled person— made me want to blend in with my background. To be part of the surroundings. To go unnoticed. I very much wanted and needed to be seen, but my comfort zone was to be unseen.

If your perception of me is an extroverted Jesus supersoldier, it's wrong. I'm a pretty quiet guy. Reaching out means I have to overcome my predispositions every time. I have to go beyond my normal into God's normal. But God *enables* me and *compels* me.

What compels me? We live in a fallen world. It was all settled on the cross, but our current reality is still fallen. Just look around. This isn't heaven yet. But maybe it could be. There are moments when the magnitude of the world's problems and pain overwhelms me. But no matter how hopeless our life in this fallen world may feel, God extends the hope of heaven to us here. Now. Today. He extends the hope of heaven through us here. "I am made all things to all men, that I might by all means save some," Paul wrote (1 Corinthians 9:22). The important word is "some." We may not be able to help everyone, but if we learn to see those we can help, opportunities for God to work in us are right in front of us.

––––––––

Let's return to expectations. They are so basic yet so key, like the deep bass tones of a symphony. Why don't we expect bubbles of heaven? I've asked myself this again and again. I have to be careful how I answer this, because I don't want to sound arrogant.

I think we've been taught not to expect them because of our ideas of so-called normal life and our faith traditions. There are entire theologies, taught by well-meaning people, dedicated to convincing folks that God's miraculous power and activity really happened "back then" in Bible times but we shouldn't expect them to happen in our lives. What?

A result of believing that such things aren't for us, that heaven is up there and we are down here, is that we've lost some of our salt and our light, some of our ability to flavor and illuminate the world with God's truth and power.

As Christians, we've become comfortable with bland lives in a bland world.

How do we live blandly? By not expecting God to work in a way that's beyond our experience. By not expecting him to bring heaven to earth all around us. When we do experience God's working in some larger way than we expect, many of us try to explain it away, call it charlatanry. The Enemy is quick to deceive us. He tries to convince us of the unreality of what is most truly real.

If we haven't seen and experienced examples of these bubbles of heaven, if we haven't noticed their patterns, then it's really hard to recognize one for the first time. They're so simple most of the time. Dismissible, like so much of God's work.

Another reason we live blandly is the microwaved, media-driven marketplace in which we live. It drives us to look for the sensational not the important. That's an omnipresent, increasing fact of Western culture in the digital age. "If it bleeds, it leads" goes the old wisdom of the news media. And a trip to a movie theater or a casual glance at social media proves that kind of thinking goes way beyond the news business. Over-the-top, in-your-face explosions, outrage, and sensations captivate our interest. It's an inverted parody of the powerful sensory qualities of heaven, the qualities we've been wired to crave. But the difference is that while every aspect of heaven's experience grounds us and forces us to live in the moment, our counterfeit priorities do just the opposite. They distract from the now and encourage numbing and escape.

Because of all this, we're distracted from the quiet works of God. The truly miraculous can often sneak past us. It's practical, simple, everyday. It's easy to dismiss. But being faithful in these small things is the path toward God's granting us larger ones. Our culture trains us to want sensationalism, but that's not how God works.

What can you do about it? For starters, you can volunteer to be God's agent in bringing heaven to earth now. Just think about the small things. Begin there. They aren't small to God. No sparrow that falls to earth escapes the notice of the Father. Who knows how important something like setting out birdseed in a Colorado winter might be to God? Who knows what God will do with the simplest actions you surrender to his will? Expect him to work. Volunteer to help. Step back and watch what happens.

"Go and do likewise," Jesus told his disciples after teaching a story about compassion (Luke 10:37, NIV). You can do this too. "Do it" is what he's saying. We don't do it in order to receive anything. We do it regardless of circumstances. We get to a point where we don't care what we get back from such encounters. God will run a million dollars through our hands if we don't have sticky fingers.

When we act on an opportunity with that kind of selfless attitude, the Father smiles. And wherever he smiles, bubbles of heaven show up. We can't experience a bubble of heaven without being changed. We will be forever different.

During my time with Jesus, he listed so many moments of my life that were important to him, but I had never given any of them a second thought. Things, interactions, words, conversations may seem small to us, but it's because we're too close to them. We don't have God's perspective. The reality is that we may never know (this side of death) which moments, words, or choices in our lives are the most important.

We may never see how we change another's life for good or bad. We may never see the impact and ripple effect of our actions. But Jesus sees every one. And he wants to work with us now to make our every action matter. We may not know how to love others the way they need to be loved, but God does. And he'll guide and use us when we volunteer for it. When we embrace that, rising above the normal expectations for what matters in this life, our lives will be forever different.

Living life at the edge of the bubbles, operating and walking through life with the expectation that God will work through us, watching for what the Father is doing and stepping into it—this life is as good as it gets on this side of heaven. I can attest to that. The lies of our hearts or culture all share the same hallmark: to distract us from our walk alongside God. The lies of money, temptation, easy living, luxury—the list is long. But all of them shrivel up and blow away when compared to the joy and glory of living with God's presence on earth. It's a taste of heaven itself. It's like seeing a preview for a movie everybody would want to star in. In fact, this life is a preview of the coming attractions of heaven. And when we get to heaven, we'll marvel at all we've experienced and realize, *Oh wow, I've felt this before.*

Trust me. It's real. And it's right here, waiting for you. It's all so much closer than you think.

13

KINGDOM OF HEAVEN BUBBLES SURPRISE US

Elaine and I took a rare trip out of the country a few years ago to follow the route of the apostle Paul's famous missionary travels. His first-century tour two thousand years ago introduced Christianity to many of the Mediterranean's most influential ancient cities, especially the city of Ephesus, which is repeatedly mentioned in the New Testament. The ruins of the city lie in a land that once belonged to the Greek empire and then the Roman empire and now is part of Turkey. We stopped there, walking where Paul had walked, amazed by the sights of a vanished civilization.

In its day Ephesus was a thriving city. A swirling center of trade, culture, and even pagan worship. A metropolis. Archaeologists have spent their careers excavating its ruins, and every time they think they've reached the boundary of the city, they uncover a wonder that sends them back to draw their maps wider. As we stood amid the remnants of so many pillars and colonnades, we thought of the ancient city as a beautiful example of the old proverb that the more you see, the less you know. The more that's uncovered, the more you realize its expanding scope.

This ancient city has become an image for my spiritual life. I have been to heaven and returned to tell about it. I have experienced healing miracles in my body that astounded my doctors, testified to God's power, and freed me from a life of disability to enjoy an active life. God has done miracles, real miracles, Bible-style miracles around me—healing others, breaking generational sin. He has provided, encouraged, and loved. But I believe these are only excavations of a tiny portion of a secret, wondrous place right under my feet, mostly unseen.

This world is like the soil of Turkey. Just beneath its surface are buried so many wonders—the story of a time and place that is here yet not here, present and right in front of us but inaccessible without God's permission. Instead of being a relic of the distant past, this is a relic of the now and of things that are to come. We don't know the surprising treasures that lie buried. We are only promised that the work of digging for them will prepare our hearts for God's presence, for the world as it should be.

For heaven.

I had the unique experience of actually walking with Jesus, hearing his voice, feeling the weight of his arm on my shoulders. Hearing specifically and lovingly the why of my entire life. It was pure love. It defined, for me, what my relationship with him should be. It defined the reason I would lay down my life gladly to follow him anywhere he might want to go. I could not stay in that place. But I left with the echoes of it inside me.

This place isn't heaven. It's fallen, scarred by sin. It doesn't look the way it's supposed to. It doesn't feel the way it's supposed to. But there are echoes of heaven all around, waiting to be noticed and to be lived.

Do you think there's a possibility you can experience the beauty and wonder of the kingdom of heaven on earth? I do.

————

To recognize heaven here, we must have the eye of a hunter so we are able to see what others ignore, notice what they walk past. There's a scene in the movie *Patch Adams* where a man in an insane asylum runs up to Robin Williams with his hand raised to his face. "How many fingers?" he asks. Williams counts and gives the obvious answer: "Four." The man storms off. Somehow the correct answer was wrong.

In a tender scene later, the truth comes out. When one's eyes are focused on the problem—looking directly at the fingers, counting them—one sees only four. When looking in the eyes of the person asking the question, though, your vision blurs. You see with both eyes.

You see eight fingers.

"Eight, eight. Yes, yes," the man says elatedly. "Eight's a good answer. Yes. See what no one else sees. See what everyone else chooses not to see. . . . See the whole world anew each day."

Seeing what others don't see. What a powerful metaphor for looking beyond ourselves.

Before I died and went to That Place, I lived the diluted

Christianity I've already mentioned in this book. I didn't know that was what I was doing, of course, and it's painful to think about now. It was orthodox and real and foundational, without question. I really had Jesus, and he really had me.

But it was diluted. This might be you. It used to be me.

I look back fondly on my religious experiences as a boy and a young man. Father Kempsel and the community of Christ the King Episcopal Church filled our house with food in a critical hour. That's clearly not diluted at all. The church and the tradition was rich. But my experience was diluted. I just didn't know what was there. My eyes hadn't been opened. Compared to my faith life after the great experience, it was thin. There was so much more to God's life than I ever dreamed. The treasures beneath my feet ran for miles. For eternity.

"The world of bland." That's the best way I can describe the world I woke up in when a navy nurse was bending over my bed. Compared to heaven, this world has no flavor. But that doesn't devalue this world. In fact, in the light of That Place, it becomes infinitely more valuable than we can even comprehend. But it is the heavenly perspective that has changed the ways I think, feel, live, love, and recognize God's work around me. God's work in me. By contrast, as good as the before was in so many ways, what came and what is still coming are so much better.

For you right now, faith may be wonderful. A source of life. But what if you were watching the world go by in grainy shades of black and white when you could be watching it in high-def color? If we were in touch with the heart of the Father, we would change.

We would behave differently. We would listen differently. We would be concerned with what he's concerned with. We would revolutionize love, and love would revolutionize us.

My time with Jesus in heaven showed me Christianity as it should be. Being with God, knowing him, being known by him—that's the goal, the end, the ultimate purpose of our entire existence. Love. That's the yearning, with everything that's in me, to go back. That's the yearning, with everything that's in me, to feel close to him here. That's the yearning—the ache, the hunger—in the deepest places of your heart, though perhaps you shirk from acknowledging it. Mine is sharper because I've had an appetizer.

Heaven is all you want once you've tasted it. I can't make God's presence come (no one can make him do anything), but that hunger for heaven keeps me alert to look for what the Father is doing here. Over the forty years of looking since I came back to life, I've seen again and again that the presence of God can never be commanded or demanded. It is always and only a pure gift. It's a pure gift to be able to see any facet, see any flash, step into any place where a bubble of heaven is forming.

God's presence? Always and only a gift. A surprising gift.

———

For years Elaine and I have sponsored children through Compassion International. We consider our Compassion kids as adopted members of our central family here in Colorado. From the jungles of Indonesia to the urban barrios of the Dominican Republic and

Honduras, we have embraced the idea of a family larger than our own.

In 2007 I was invited to be part of a vision trip to Colombia. Part of my background in international economics includes the area of economic development. Part of my work there was to help create a multilateral, multilayered financial architecture that would provide for deep, sustainable development. I was thankful my schooling and experience might benefit others. Little did I know I was the one about to get a real education!

Part of the trip was to travel from the developed city center of Cartagena to one of the Compassion centers for development located within the barrio. The organizers of the trip were emphatic that we should bring work clothes, including boots, to the development center. Thick-soled hiking boots were particularly encouraged.

I received a lesson of a lifetime within the barrio.

A small group of us were invited into the home of the Cardenases—a family sponsored by Compassion. This is an unusual family. First, the head of the household is a man, unlike most of the families we met, which were matriarchal. Second, despite living in the middle of the barrio, they have one of the nicer homes. The three-room house has a corrugated metal roof and dirt floors. When it rains, the family stays dry, unlike many of their neighbors.

The sanitation system is simply a network of depressions in the middle of the streets through which raw sewage flows downhill into the nearby lagoon. Rain is required to "flush" the depressions and "refresh" the lagoon. When it does not rain, the raw sewage simply sits. As our visit was during the dry season and it had not rained for many days, I now understood the need for thick-soled boots. We walked through the streets fighting hard to keep breakfast down.

The Cardenases were fortunate to have electricity. A makeshift wire snaked around the corner of the roof, down the wall to a light-bulb socket with a dim incandescent light bulb. Below the light bulb was an improvised table with a cinder-block chair. On the table was an open, worn Bible. I got a little weak in the knees—not from the stench outside but from the bubble of the kingdom of heaven now forming inside—so I staggered to sit on the bed in the room. The three Cardenas kids all rushed me, fighting to see who could get the best seat on the lap of "their" sponsor. In reality, I wasn't their sponsor. The only similarity was the color of my skin. Only one of the kids had a Compassion sponsor, which meant at least one of them would get one good, nutritious meal each day (and the three kids often traded off). All three attended the development center on the Compassion grounds, ensuring that they were safe during the day. Not even the gangs will cross that boundary.

I hugged all three children until they wouldn't take any more and then pointed to the open Bible and asked the translator if he could get some answers from the kids' father. The translator explained, "He is a laborer, fit and healthy. It is his calling . . . out of necessity."

Through the translator, Mr. Cardenas said, "Every morning

before sunrise I get up, turn on the light, and read God's Word. I am so blessed to have light to read by. We have three locations within the barrio where we laborers can go to be selected for work, so I ask God where I should go. I get there early. Sometimes I get work, sometimes not. Sometimes I get good work. When that happens, we have extra to share. Many here are not as well off as we are. God provides us what we need. You are part of that provision."

Because of his vocation, sometimes he has provisions to share. Rather than stuffing the extra into a coffee can, he gives it to his neighbors. Simple community. God's provision shared.

The bubble of heaven popped as we stepped back into the street. Somehow the stench wasn't as bad now. Looking back, I wondered if the Cardenas family lived in a bubble of heaven routinely. Routinely enough for daily provision. Daily bread. The kingdom of heaven in a barrio of Colombia? Who would have thought? It was certainly a surprise to me.

I wrote in my journal during the flight back: "I wonder how the Father in heaven defines poverty. Is it possible the Cardenases are actually rich and I am really poor in God's eyes? Why do I worry about the next business transaction when I could just as easily sit in my womb room and be guided by a loving Father into discovering my vocation?" (I have a quiet room set apart in my house for spiritual rest and meeting God. Because it helps me be nourished and grow, like a little child, I call it my "womb room.")

Through the Holy Spirit, we have a new deal. New guidance. Everybody matters. We all have power from God, given so we can give to others. You're not the one picked last for the baseball team. No one is. We're all part of God's starting lineup.

You are important. You. I am important. We all are important. If we realize that, we can relax. We can begin to know the specifics of the purpose that God has made us for, and we can embrace it with joy, steering all the resources he has given us in that holy direction.

"You're on my team," God says. *"You're chosen."*

———————

I am a fellow traveler on this journey.

It's taken a long time for me to grow, for me to get to this point where I believe I have something to share. Something meaningful, edifying, worthwhile. I am not an expert, but I am learning to invite God daily, to make myself available. I see a progression in my faith and ability to know heaven's presence on earth as I look back over the thirty to forty years between now and my two experiences. I have a sense of growth, which continues today. Often through struggle.

As I have grown to embrace the idea that the kingdom of heaven is actually near in our day-to-day lives, I have learned to see facets of heaven and make conscious decisions to step into the bubbles that form. When I do, I know and perceive I am on holy ground. I am treading in the thin places where God is making his love known in the midst of our earthly struggles. He cares. *"It's okay,"* he says at such moments, sometimes through miracles and sometimes through the simplest means. These flashes, as I move toward them, happen more frequently. The bubbles last longer. They are frequently full of surprises.

But to be honest, some of those lessons have come with difficulty. Here's one example of why we need to be sensitive, wise, and strategic about how we approach joining moments when God seems to be doing something.

We did an event at our house for a group of Christian men I'm close to. It was a celebration of what God is doing among us. The group and their spouses gathered in our home. I had just had a dream about the wife of one of the members—even though I had never seen her or met her before. In the dream I saw that something about her was broken. Simply broken. What came to my mind was that God wanted to set her right. As I said, I had never met her, knew nothing at all about her or her history. When she came into our house, I recognized her immediately and exactly as the woman from my dream.

"Do I look familiar to you?" I asked her curiously.

"Well, no," she answered. I learned that she had a serious back problem and was in debilitating pain. Permanent, omnipresent pain. She had been living with pain and was constantly medicated for pain. It was as if the pain had become part of her. Later we had some time over coffee to talk, and I shared that I had dreamed about her.

After the meeting her husband, a pastor, said, "She's a little wigged out that someone she doesn't know had a dream about her the night before she came over."

She was very uncomfortable, and I certainly can't blame her.

It might have been off-putting for anyone. I apologized. "I didn't handle that well," I admitted.

The last thing I wanted to do was freak anyone out. I had no doubt that God was working through the dream, that something was important there. But I was insensitive to the situation, and the person I was intended to connect with was understandably taken aback by my awkward approach. I still believe there's an important connection, perhaps a bubble of heaven waiting to form. But I'm also still learning how to handle such moments. I pray that God gives me another chance to pray with her and see what the Father has in mind. A chance to play a little part in bringing the kingdom into a place of chronic physical pain.

In hindsight, I realize I should have entered a sensitive situation like that by asking more questions, by carefully feeling out the situation and listening for God's guidance before saying anything that might upset her. I should have worked more to understand the traditions and beliefs in her background, her framework for thinking about God. Just because we are given insight doesn't mean that it's supposed to be used immediately.

I believe situations like this are part of "our growing in use." We learn. We make mistakes. That's okay. But with that said, such moments when bubbles might be forming are usually places of tremendous vulnerability and, in a sense, danger. They wouldn't be important if they weren't. But just as there is incredible power to heal at such moments, similarly there is incredible power to wound or hurt if something goes wrong. The responsibility isn't all on us, but we need to be hand in glove with the Father through the personal guidance system of the Holy Spirit. Leaning on our own understanding can be very tempting and very dangerous. We must not depend on ourselves. We must depend on the Spirit. The minute you think this is a self thing, you're lost in the deep woods.

In light of this, my prayer has become: *Dear Lord, please make me sharper, a tool in your hand. Not dull.*

My ultimate goal is that people feel loved by me at a cellular level, that they experience the love of the Father through me. That is the goal. I can't own the results, but if the process is love, I can own that.

I'm more available now than I've ever been. I'm quicker to recognize the Spirit's leading and the Father's presence than I've ever been. I have so far to go, but I have come so far too, and that is a journey for God's glory and a witness to his faithfulness and patience.

Like excavating a buried city, the more I see, the more I *can* see.

———

My dream story alone should convince you that this isn't just for the perfect, for the person who always knows what to do. I've made my share of mistakes. I'm walking a bumpy road like anyone.

But I am convinced of this: surely heaven on earth is for the learners, for the mistake makers like me. Surely this isn't just for me. Surely you don't need to spend weeks lying unresponsive in a hospital bed in order to recognize God's presence in this world. I may have needed it to recognize God's power, to know what it feels like to be in his presence, but I believe in the very depths of my heart that you and I and everyone can live like this now. It's a vision that's meant to multiply. This is a pathway, a different way to live. It is a road for all of us.

I'm still learning to see. Still learning to apply myself to this. Still on a journey of discovery. But I believe in my heart that it can be your journey too.

Isn't that good news? You don't have to be a pastor or have a PhD in theology to get this. It's accessible. To everyone. It's really simple when you boil it down. My death showed me this. So has my life after heaven.

This is a flash of the kingdom:

- It's God's will being done in a truck-stop diner as it is in heaven.
- It's God's will being done in Wal-Mart or in a supermarket checkout line or at the office as it is in heaven.
- It's God's will being done in church or in a former liquor store as it is in heaven.
- It's God's will being done in our calendars as it is in heaven.
- It's God's will being done in our hearts and minds and families and wallets as it is in heaven.

- It's God's will being done everywhere as it is in heaven.
- It's God's will being done in me and in you as it is in heaven.

If this is true, the kingdom of heaven is a revolution that will quietly overthrow the world. See, this is for regular folks, people who want to love Jesus but don't think of themselves as particularly spiritual, every bit as much as it is for veteran, mature Christians. Because the worth, power, and specialness of this life lies entirely with the Father, we are free not to have to carry those burdens ourselves. He makes everything worthwhile. All we bring is our willingness to be used. Our lives.

So, in one of those pesky heavenly paradoxes, we bring nothing to God or his work. And at the same time, we bring everything.

God gives complete access to every one of us, regardless of circumstances, regardless of whether we are someone worthy or seen in the eyes of the world. This isn't like spiritual pole-vaulting or skydiving. He includes everyone in his Son's mission to bring heaven to earth. Anyone can be part of it. Anyone. I am living proof.

What I am talking about is not just an external spiritual activity limited to habits you put on or take off like a raincoat. They're habits you ingest. They become part of you, internally, and begin to change you from the inside out. Don't you want that too? Consider for a moment. Don't you want to live so surrendered to the Father's will that your very insides change? Don't you want life to be an adventure of waiting—significant, meaningful waiting—to see what God will do next and how he will use you?

I can only tell you, wow, it's worth living for!

Don't you want to volunteer?

But isn't there a cost to all this? I've done a lot of thinking about the scriptures that address the cost of discipleship. Yes, there's a cost to all this—and a big one. How do we vanquish and overcome the fears of that cost? After all, Jesus's call for us to live as citizens of the kingdom of heaven now will cost us everything. Look at his teachings in the Gospels. Again and again he talks about dying so we can live. There's nothing costlier than dying. I know. And it's appropriate to talk about cost.

What will this cost?

Everything.

My advantage is that I'm already playing with house money. I'm living on borrowed time. Heaven's dime. Heaven's time. I've died, for heaven's sake. I've been there and back again. Everything has a totally different meaning for me now. And I would trade everything—everything!—in an instant to return to heaven.

It's easy for me to count the cost because I've already tasted the benefits. I've been given a powerful peek at the reward God gives to his children. Been there. Done that. Going there again. I continue to receive those benefits one bubble at a time.

Do we all need to have a near-death experience to overcome the fear of giving God the totality of our lives, time, and resources?

To give him our fears of loss? of suffering? of death? To say to him that we are truly his, not our own, and that he can do with us as he sees fit?

The answer is no.

He wants us to live in his presence now. In this life. In whatever place we live, whatever activities fill our lives.

My encouragement is this: whatever the cost will be for you to live this way, it's worth it. It's why my death is worth living for. To teach that the kingdom of heaven is much closer than we think, much closer than we've been led to believe. To teach that we live in a diluted world, and it's the Father's heart—his intimate desire—that we live in a present that is rich and potent with his presence. Undiluted.

Remember that God invited Solomon to make a request of him. When Solomon asked for wisdom, the Father gave him wisdom—and included everything else in the package. Take it from a financial advisor. That's a pretty good investment.

Whatever the cost is, the other side of the ledger is of so much greater weight. There's no comparison. But the Adversary, the Deceiver, the Enemy readily puts us in a place where we react to the tangibility of cost in order to keep us from the intangible (for now) reward offered by the Father. It's part of the price he paid for his Son.

There's a relationship offered through the Holy Spirit that's exceptionally tangible. He is here with us. That is my encouragement. My reminder of the future waiting for me at the end of the white tunnel.

This is all wrapped up with two stories Jesus told—the parables of the hidden treasure and the pearl of great price. He said in Matthew 13:44–46 (ESV):

The kingdom of heaven is like treasure hidden in a field, which a man found and covered up. Then in his joy he goes and sells all that he has and buys that field.

Again, the kingdom of heaven is like a merchant in search of fine pearls, who, on finding one pearl of great value, went and sold all that he had and bought it.

The man sold everything because of the great value of the treasure here. It cost him everything to buy the field. But he got everything back. The same with the merchant.

It's like Solomon, who asked for wisdom. God gave it to him but threw in all the good and tempting things that Solomon didn't ask for. You see, if we get God, if we get the Father's heart, if we get heaven, we come out infinitely ahead, no matter what we lose. He's all we need.

If I need God and (fill in the blank), then something is wrong. He is enough, and he needs to be enough. He is sufficient. I will take nothing else back with me when I return to heaven. I don't get to take anything except the love of God. Everything else is left here. It's like the last scene of the movie *Ghost*. Sam says, "It's amazing, Molly. The love inside, you take it with you." (Hollywood got the theology right on that one.)

You know when you're out of alignment with the Father's will and ways. You feel pressure, stress, a distance from the Father that is terrible—the opposite of heaven. The opposite of patience, peace, presence, pure joy. You feel spiritually that you're not where you need to be. *Lord, help me get back in alignment with you* is my prayer at such moments.

There is still room for wilderness experiences here though, times when our spiritual journeys are not necessarily pleasant, but we're not as far from God as we may feel. These are preparation times. Mine primarily came, intensively, during the ten years between my first experience of heaven and my second. But as you grow, you keenly feel any degree of separation from the Father. It disturbs and unsettles you. You feel in your bones that it's not how things should be. There are times when the Father is silent. But he is never absent. He does not leave or forsake us.

I'm constantly aware that I—that any of us—can be sinning, outside God's will, and be totally unaware of it. Sometimes it's through ignorance. Sometimes through self-deception. But it's very real. Being aware of this should create mindfulness, a constant turning to God. I ask him to reveal to me the truth and meaning of my actions from his heavenly perspective, which I have heard firsthand is so different from my own.

May the Divine Guide, the Divine Instructor, keep all of us where he wants us to be. May he keep us on a short leash and not allow us to wander into the ditch. He does that in community, but he does that sovereignly and mysteriously as well. This is all an element of what I am continuing to learn in this process. I'm growing. And I'm willing to continue to grow.

We're only uncovering the barest bit of these deep and wonderful mysteries. This is the very heart of the Father, depthless like the universe. In the face of that, I feel my smallness. That humble recognition is not hard to come by when we realize God's greatness and our not-so-greatness. People become humbler with every true encounter they have with the Father. Why? Because in seeing him for who he really is, we see ourselves for who we really are.

But the truth is that the mysteries don't always reveal themselves the way we'd choose. Everyone likes to see wins, visible miracles, instantly changed lives. Sometimes that's what God does. But a lot of times it isn't.

I have asked for hundreds of healings that did not happen. I have prayed thousands of specific prayers that were not granted the way I ached to see. God's perspective is so much bigger than mine. And I trust that, in light of a conversation with Jesus, every one of those things was better, from heaven's perspective, not to be done in my way.

Oh, my friend, every time I see the kingdom impact people, it takes me back to being in heaven. It's like a heavenly filling station. It's pure nourishment for my still-raw soul. That feeling feeds me in a way nothing else does. It continues to change me. I'm a different person every time I encounter a bubble of heaven. We may not be the primary recipients of a bubble—we're God's agents after all, volunteers. But we can't help but benefit.

And that's just a sliver of the glorious hope of heaven. It is so much more than pink cherub harpists or puffy clouds or pearly gates. It is intimacy with the Creator, the Father of the universe himself. Unity. Perfect, personal love.

And this kind of intimacy with God is for everyone. It is for you.

God's surprising invitation to bring heaven to earth is waiting all around us, ready to break into our bland reality with power and clarity. It's there, everywhere, just as his loving presence is. I ache for you to see it and feel it, for you to gain a taste of the glorious reality that awaits you whenever you take your last breath and step into That Place and walk with Jesus yourself. An encounter with heaven changes lives. I am living proof.

My death has been so very worth living for.

And I can't wait to see what you will do with it.

14

KINGDOM OF
HEAVEN BUBBLES
ARE OPPORTUNITIES

Years ago I had a dream. I am standing in line in front of the classic (and not quite right) image of Saint Peter at the entrance to heaven. The people in front of me go up one by one and hand Peter an envelope. He has a little wooden box on his podium, and for each person, he shuffles through it, finds something in there, and hands it to them. The people pass on by and march into heaven.

Finally it's my turn. In my dream I'm totally confused by what's going on. I walk up to Peter, wondering what to do.

"You have a CD in your pocket," he says.

Sure enough, I do.

"It's everything you did on earth," he said.

I immediately fall to my knees, ready to beg for God's forgiveness. Peter laughs.

"No, we don't do that here," he said. "That's all been taken care of."

Now I'm doubly confused.

Peter flips through the wooden box and pulls out another CD. "This is everything you were intended to do."

It was not a list of sins but a list of the good things that might have been. The potential we each carried. In my dream I am overcome with a longing that the two CDs match. What if my life lived up to the full potential for good that God desired for me? What if I did all the good things God wanted me to do?

Saint Peter holding a CD is a humorous picture. But I'm just crazy enough to want the point of that dream to be true. I beg God not to let me miss a single opportunity to do what I'm intended to do. *Make me alert,* I pray. *Make all your people alert to do what you intend for us to do. In all these things, to God be the glory.*

————

A number of years ago Elaine was preparing one of her culinary masterpieces when she discovered some of the ingredients she'd been saving for this meal had already been eaten. (This happens with teenagers in the house.) She asked if I'd be willing to make a Saturday-morning grocery run. *Sigh.*

I usually do not shop for groceries. I especially do not shop on a Saturday in King Soopers, the local supermarket chain. But Elaine is the love of my life.

"Of course, dear! I would love to go to King Soopers for you. Will you make a list?" I replied. (I was scoring major marriage points.)

I had seven items to find on this search-and-secure mission. But I was having trouble finding what she needed. Halfway through my shopping, a six- or seven-year-old boy caught my eye. He'd somehow ditched his mom. This little guy was dressed in a camouflage T-shirt and denim pants that had not seen the inside of a washing machine in a while. His hair was disheveled, as if he'd been rousted out of bed and transported straight to the store. In short, he was my kind of kid. I loved him instantly, thinking back to when I was the boy behind the hungry eyes.

He and I were playing peekaboo among the pumpkins in the produce section when his mother appeared. She grabbed his arm with a vise grip and shoved her face inches from his and growled through clenched teeth, "Haven't I told you not to play with strangers!"

I'd encroached on her parental turf. She half-walked, half-dragged her son up the aisle as fast as she could. She wanted to put distance between her son and me. The camo-clad cherub continued to look over his shoulder. He gave a weak wave with his free hand, and his eyes silently said, *Bye-bye, strange stranger. It was fun while it lasted.*

After I finished my scavenger hunt for the remainder of the items on Elaine's list, I arrived at the checkout lane to find the little boy in his mother's arms right in front of me. With a big grin and bright eyes, he tugged on her sleeve and pointed. She looked at me and glared.

Then I noticed her shopping cart. No one could feed a family with that meager amount of food. There was a whole story in front of me, and it appeared to include hunger. I knew what it was like to be a kid without food in the house.

That same emotional explosion I had in the pancake place so many years prior went off in my heart again. "Excuse me," I said to her. "Did you get everything you needed to pick up today?"

Surprised by the question, she replied, "No, we are a little short this week."

"Not today. Not on my watch." I replied. The clerk had already started the *beep, beep, beep* process of running her items through the checkout system. "Get another cart and finish your list. Your groceries are on me today."

"All of it?" she asked incredulously.

"Whatever you need." I said.

She hesitated for a second and then handed her son to me as she dashed off to get another cart. The mother, unable to properly feed her family, overcame her worry of handing off her son to a strange stranger. A bubble that felt like heaven formed around us and expanded to engulf the surrounding area.

I turned to the cashier. "You might want to shut off your light. This could take a while."

She reached over without a word and flicked the toggle switch. Tears fell on the conveyor belt as she straightened back up, her hand not quick enough to catch them. The bubble had enveloped her as well.

I leaned back to the burly guy behind me with a loaded cart. "I'm sorry. You might want to change lines."

"Not on your life," he said. "I want to watch this and see how it plays out." He was perhaps a bit misty too, catching the edge of the bubble.

The three of us chatted until the mom returned from a twenty-minute shopping spree with a cart loaded to the top. The entire time felt to me like being back in heaven.

I've reared three boys. Unless they were sick or asleep, they hardly sat still for anything. But my little camo friend clung to me for dear life the entire time. He didn't look around, didn't fidget like little boys are supposed to. He just hugged me. Only when his mom returned did he loosen his grip.

The *beep, beep, beep* started again. The cashier wept the entire time. The man behind me had a case of the sniffles. One large grocery bill later (it's all God's money anyhow) a speechless mom hugged a strange stranger. Her tears did all the talking. The boy in the camo T-shirt beamed as he followed her out of the store. He looked over his shoulder and waved as they left.

I had never seen that mother and her boy before, and I've not seen them since. To this day I wonder if that little boy wasn't Jesus in the flesh, hugging someone who really needed it. That alone was worth the money. At least, it was for me that day.

You don't expect to find the kingdom in a grocery store, do you? But it was paradise for twenty minutes. We were inside a bubble of heaven.

———

Heaven intersects all aspects of our lives here. We just need to learn to recognize it. The easiest to recognize are the spiritual aspects—those moments in worship or prayer when the presence and power of God are palpable. That is like heaven, but just here. But the same power and presence easily felt at those moments extend into all aspects of life. It can be vocational (heaven experienced in our work and calling). It can be physical (heaven experienced through healing, for instance). It can be financial (heaven operating to great capacity in a soul that's generous and faithful with resources).

There aren't recipes for these kinds of experiences—only a relationship, a path to follow. Only the creation of an expectation for God to work here as he does there. For us to be mentally and emotionally open to a relationship with the triune God. For his presence to be made known to us. For his power to be revealed. For our lives—and the world around us—to be changed.

Here's the thing though: the minute we try to control the results of a situation, it all collapses. I began to understand why. Trying to control results is a slip backward into religion, not the life of faith. The outcome of any situation belongs to God and God alone. I pray for him to keep me from deceiving myself, from subtly wandering into the territory meant for his influence.

There's more that we should be experiencing in the here and now. Our expectations are far too low. Heaven is much closer than we think. The heart of the Father is a lot closer to us than we think. In all of life, open up your mind. Open up your soul.

Our culture and world are emotionally compromised. We don't know how to feel the way God feels, and it impairs all of life.

We've been taught to encapsulate ourselves in whatever protective device we can devise, to insulate our vulnerabilities. This isn't heaven's way. It only imprisons us. God forgive us for doing this to ourselves. Because when we do that, we close ourselves off to the greatest depths of faith and life. We close ourselves off to the things of God.

How did we get here? Gradually. Little bit by little bit until we think our experience is normal, simply the way human life is meant to be. But that's so far from the truth.

It's not how it's supposed to be. That's not how we're supposed to live. There is an alternative. The way God truly meant for us to live is in deep, shared communion with him and our neighbors. This doesn't mean we'll never suffer. We certainly will. Nor does it mean our lives are all sunshine and naive happiness. That's not how things work.

What it means is that God's intent for us is to live here on earth in a way that foreshadows heaven.

What it means is that no matter how we feel, abundant life and love and joy are all around us, whether we see them or not.

And God wants to use you and me to help them become visible.

Things will be different now. I now carry that feeling with me in every moment of my life. I fill my lungs with sweet life-giving air and think of the relief, the joy, the true inspiration of it all. Jesus was right—things have been different. Very different!

———

Let me return to the story of Chuck, the first person I ever told about my experience in heaven and who found heaven at work in a Wal-Mart.

By the end of his time at the store, they were paying him a fair wage, but he wasn't there for the money. He was there because he had found paradise. He was loved and loving. Used by God over and over again. Close to the Father. The years passed. And Chuck went from an elderly Wal-Mart greeter to an old Wal-Mart greeter.

Then cancer got the best of him. Chuck died.

I now have Chuck's blue Wal-Mart vest. That "stupid old vest" he talked about. It's one of my most prized possessions today. Chuck left it to me in his will. And the general manager of his store had to sign off on letting that little piece of company property leave the store.

Chuck was an orthodox Episcopalian at fifty-three, and he died an orthodox Episcopalian at seventy-three. He loved the high church, the Advent ceremonies, the structure and beauty of the liturgical church year. And at the same time, he stood at the front of a Wal-Mart store for twenty years and hugged everybody who walked in.

Chuck was my dad.

Yes, Chuck was my father, the often-out-of-work dad I remember from my boyhood.

Two times I saw my father cry at a table. The first, which I mentioned in chapter 1, was when there was no food in our house and he was out of work. He couldn't do it. He couldn't provide for his own needs, let alone those of his family. The second was in that little breakfast joint after he told me God had given him a job. Then he shed tears of joy at realizing God himself was meeting him over and over again in the aisles at work. Those two memories are poignant for me.

I gave the eulogy at my father's funeral. I work in finance. He ended up working in retail. But I spoke of sharing a family business with him: looking for bubbles, flashes of heaven in the world around us.

Half of the people in that packed church remembering my dad were folks from Wal-Mart—employees and customers alike. My dad's death was a moment of witness for them. More than one expressed not understanding where Dad's love had come from until they understood his love for God.

If that's not a taste of heaven, I don't know what is. Even if it was wrapped in a blue Wal-Mart vest.

If an unemployed fifty-three-old orthodox Episcopalian—a man no one would even interview after a lifetime of vocational wandering—could find heaven as close as his workplace, under fluorescent lights and over white linoleum, what about you? Whatever your life station, what about you?

Wherever you happen to be—worker, unemployed, student. Far beyond the categories of secular and sacred, I think all of us are already part of the kingdom of heaven. Here on earth. Is it possible we can be enlisted in the service of That Place while we're still living in this one? Yes. It's more than possible. Guys, gals, ladies, gentlemen, it's all sacred. God makes it sacred.

The kingdom of heaven is at hand. I live it. Chuck, my dad, lived it.

You can too. The joy of it is that you can choose the path.

EPILOGUE

In 2015 I was in Los Angeles for a Christian conference. One of the stories from the podium was very similar to mine. The woman speaking had had a major medical problem, had gone to heaven, wasn't allowed to stay. As I listened, I understood that the speaker had experienced this fairly recently, only a year or two before. I thought it was unfortunate they were publicly highlighting her so soon. Just looking at her, I could tell she was still reeling from the experience.

I sought her out afterward. I gently took her by the arm and said a couple of things that rocked her world—things that only someone who had been there would know and understand.

"How did you know?" she asked. "I haven't said anything about those details to anyone. Not even my husband."

"We're kindred spirits," I replied. "Forty years ago I was where you are right now."

People often don't know what to do with stories such as mine—stories of white tunnels and a white-robed Jesus. Stories of the "life review" that makes sense of all of one's pain. Stories of outright miracles, of healings, of dreams that are more than dreams, but also warnings and signs and insights into the secret hearts of other people.

I understand that skepticism and empathize. Our world often makes it difficult to believe there is the possibility of another one. What's more, human nature is always quick to sensationalize and sell the holy if it cannot dismiss it. (I'm not sure whether disbelief or commercialization is more dangerous.)

But my firm belief is that we who have seen the other side have no need to prove heaven exists, to convince anyone of anything. We, instead, need to live heaven on earth, or the entire experience—however gripping and best-selling the story might be—was really for not much of anything. How will this affect us here and now? That is the question we have to answer.

We all have a burden to encourage heaven to break into our world now. I have been there, but what does that mean here? That's the most important question I, or any of us, can ask. What does that experience mean to me? What does it mean to the hurting and the broken? What does it mean to you?

So often Christians talk about faith as if it's an academic exercise instead of a relational experience. We need to tell people the who of God, how he is interested, invested, gloriously obsessed with being present, with working intimately in our lives today. This is about building a relationship with the risen Christ. His presence doesn't have to wait until you die.

God himself yearns for you on the other side, saying "Come," desiring to draw you to himself. There is a groaning of God for us, only heightened by the brutality and suffering on earth. Just in my corner of the financial world (the usury, the dishonesty, the exploitation, the lack of ethics)—God yearns to make it all right. Every week I read something in the *Wall Street Journal* about people brazenly and remorselessly admitting to terrible, harmful, greedy practices. "We did this, so sue us," they say in essence. God's nostrils flare at that. And then there's the human trafficking, the atrocities we perpetrate against one another. Violence. Injustice. Terrorism. Abuse. God himself aches over all these. Jesus weeps over them. He hurts over such things.

The evil of this fallen world is the result of the Deceiver. The Enemy. God hates it. As earth becomes less like heaven, the Father increasingly groans, longs to make it anew as he has promised in the Bible. I need to decrease—we all need to decrease—so the Father can increase here. I want to become more like his Son. I want to think like the Son. To breathe like him. To feel like him. Here. So that I might be useful. Here.

Guide me, Lord. Use me. I volunteer.

"I'm a fool for Christ. Whose fool are you?" says the old bumper sticker. There's truth to that. I'm willing to take the slings and arrows of the Enemy, of the mess that is humanity. They say I'm just another religious lunatic. But I'm willing to take it all for the richness that I know and feel already and that I will know and feel again when I return permanently to the Father's home.

The reward is there, and it's wonderful, but I don't do it for that reason. It's not a kind of transaction. The success theologies are all bogus. I do what I do for love. For the presence and joy of God. Heaven is his. Earth is his. Their mixture is his.

I am his and so are you.

My hope is that you do not see this book as a memoir or a literary work but as a reference manual. A fellow traveler's guidebook on our shared journey of following Jesus. My prayer for you is that you will go forth with the anticipation—not the expectation—that the Father will show you the bubbles of heaven. May those bubbles expand in your spaces. May you get a taste of the kingdom come on earth as it is in heaven.

If that happens, then my death, my long years of disability and suffering, every difficulty and challenge and joy in my life— all of that, *all* of that—will have been worth living for.

Why?

Because the Father made it heaven.

AFTERWORD

This world is not heaven, and I have a front-row seat to that truth in the lives of so many women.

Imagine being kidnapped, drugged, taken to another place, and handed over against your will to an evil master who sells your body for sex. How in the world could you ever get free, not only of your restraints, but of the trauma that will surely haunt you for the rest of your life?

Such stories are a reality for so many women in my world. I founded Hope Ranch to respond directly to the needs of women in the brutal aftermath of human trafficking. We create pathways to freedom for people incarcerated by that world. We have been called heaven on earth, which brings me to Steve Musick, a man who has worked alongside us here. (You read the Hope Ranch story in chapter 11.)

Steve Musick is in the aftermath of his own profound and unchosen experience, though one very far from the reality of trafficking. Imagine the difficulty of integrating into life here after that kind of experience! One might expect that a man living in the aftermath of going to heaven would be, perhaps, relationally challenged. Steve isn't. In fact, that experience now informs his life and ministry, helping make this earth a little bit more like heaven. Steve is an integral part of Hope Ranch. When he visits, there is always a sense of anticipation. We are excited simply to spend time with him. But every time he comes, he also leaves more of the tangibility of the fact that the kingdom of heaven is expanding on this earth here and now.

Steve's dedication to bringing heaven here is evident to everyone at Hope Ranch. He encourages us to be an extension of the hands of God to the women we serve. He was with us before our main location was even operational. We walked together through the membrane of one of the so-called bubbles of heaven he talks about. It's true! Ask the women who have been rescued from a horrific life in bondage as sex slaves. It takes the kingdom of heaven to have this change occur at Hope Ranch. Steve sensed the specialness of this place and these people in our early stages. He recognized a little bit of heaven, and he has been helping to expand it ever since.

Over the years I have come to know Steve. I have seen the consistency of his character and the dedication of his life to make his death worth living for. He is a joy to be around.

At Hope Ranch it is life changing to operate as if heaven is closer than we think. I encourage you to invite that kind of paradigm change, the one that Steve shares throughout this book.

I understand the extreme difficulty of eradicating evils such as human trafficking. And with that understanding, I believe Steve's life message can be applied in every dimension of any life. Part of making his death worth living for is his seeing you now live your life in light of heaven.

Live now according to your divine calling. What are you

called to become? Find your own calling in the life of a man whose death has been so worth living for.

Cathy Turner, founder and curator,

Hope Ranch, Wichita, Kansas

ACKNOWLEDGMENTS

This book has been a collaboration of many people without whom this work would never have been written. A heartfelt thank-you goes out to the following:

To my first family: Elaine, Jarrod, Brett, and Aaron.

To my second family: all the Destiny Capital team who graciously arranged time for me to pursue this endeavor.

To my other second family: Tracy and Ed, Diana and Josh, and Marcia and Wes.

To my faith family at Christ Community Covenant Church.

To my prayer team: Wes, Judy, Jake, Hannah, and Ed.

To my Wichita faith family at Eastside Community Church and Hope Ranch. You saw this effort in practice even before it became a literary work. The kingdom of heaven is at hand in the here and now within your midst.

To Paul and Emily, who are clearly with every aspect of this work and my life now.

To the team at WaterBrook, who took a huge risk on a never-before-published author with no platform for marketing. May your risk be rewarded thirty-, sixty-, a hundredfold.

To mentor Wes. 'Til death do us part.

Finally, a relationship with the Father, Son, and Holy Spirit built the life evident in these pages. They want a relationship with you to build into your lives as well.

TRANSFORM YOUR LIFE
ON EARTH TODAY

This is your opportunity to engage with
Steve and learn how to experience the
kingdom of heaven in the here and now.

Join the conversation at SteveMusick.com

WATERBROOK

www.waterbrookmultnomah.com